MERRILL

Health

Focus
on
You

Linda Meeks, M.S.

Associate Professor of Health Education
College of Education
The Ohio State University
Columbus, Ohio

Philip Heit, Ed.D.

Professor and Chairman of Health Education
Professor of Allied Medicine
College of Education   College of Medicine
The Ohio State University, Columbus, Ohio

Cover Photograph
You make many choices each day. You
choose how you will spend your time.
You may choose how you will spend
your money. It is important to make
wise choices when spending money.
These boys are choosing a gift for a
friend. They are thinking carefully
about how best to spend their money.

MERRILL
PUBLISHING COMPANY

Columbus, Ohio

A Merrill Health Program

Health: *Focus on You®,* K Big Book (with TE)
Health: *Focus on You®,* Student Editions, 1–8
Health: *Focus on You®,* Teacher Editions, 1–8
Health: *Focus on You®,* Teacher Resource Books, K–8 (Reproducible Masters)
Transparency Package (K-8)
Health Directory

Linda Meeks and **Philip Heit** are the coauthors of Merrill Publishing Company's K to 12 health program. Ms. Meeks and Dr. Heit conduct workshops in health science, curriculum design, and health methodology, in addition to the courses they teach at The Ohio State University. Both have taught health education in public schools and have individually authored articles and texts. Ms. Meeks is coauthor of *Toward a Healthy Lifestyle Through Elementary Health Education.* Ms. Meeks and Dr. Heit are the coauthors of *Teaching Health in Middle and Secondary Schools.*

Editorial Review Board

Consultants

Robert T. Brown, M.D.
Associate Professor of Clinical Pediatrics
Director of Adolescent Medicine
The Ohio State University
Columbus, OH

Gus T. Dalis, Ed.D.
Consultant, Health Education
Los Angeles County Office of Education
Downey, CA

Dale Evans, H.S.D.
Associate Professor and
Director of Teacher Training
University of Houston
Houston, TX

Florence M. Fenton, Ed.D.
Supervisor of Health Services
Prince George's County Public Schools
Upper Marlboro, MD

Todd F. Holzman, M.D.
Senior Child Psychiatrist
Harvard Community Health Plan
Wellesley, MA

Ann Shelton, Ph.D.
District Health Specialist
Portland Public Schools
Portland, OR

Reviewers

Deborah Dell D'Annunzio
Health/Drug Education Specialist
West Palm Beach, FL

Alice Payne
Ruidoso Public Schools
Ruidoso, NM

Janet C. Pearson
Kammerer Middle School
Jefferson County Public Schools
Louisville, KY

Michael R. Schiavi
Health Coordinator
Lackawanna City School District
Lackawanna, NY

Karen Spellman
Omaha Public Schools
Omaha, NE

Donna Taigen
Christian Center School
Dublin, CA

Content Specialists

Lynne E. Kahn, Ph.D.
District Coordinator of
Health Education, K-12
White Plains Public Schools
White Plains, NY

John D. Mahilo, D.D.S.
Dental Health Consultant
Gahanna, OH

Richard C. Rapp
Chemical Dependence Counselor
Wright State University
Dayton, OH

Patricia A. Weber
Nutrition Education Consultant
Hinsdale, IL

Stuart Weibel, Ph.D.
Substance Abuse Consultant
Dublin, OH

Project Editor: Rashelle R. Thraen; *Editors:* Teri A. Curtis, Nerma C. Henderson, H. Addison Lynes, Robin P. Mahaffey, Linda McLaughlin, Debra L. Sommers, Jennifer Whittingham; *Production Editors:* Helen Mischka, Jillian Yerkey; *Project Designer:* Jeff Kobelt; *Project Artist:* Lisa Russell; *Artist:* Christine F. Rodock; *Photo Editor:* Mark Burnett; *Cover Photo Editor:* Barbara Buchholz; *Illustrators:* 158 Street Design Group; Dick Smith

Cover Photo Credit: George Anderson

ISBN 0-675-03253-9

Published by

Merrill Publishing Company

Columbus, Ohio

For You

Everyone needs to know how to make responsible decisions for good health. As you use *Health: Focus on You*®, you will study about health. You will study how to make healthful choices.

You may have questions about health. What are drugs? Why is exercise important? How can I say NO when someone asks me to do something harmful? *Health: Focus on You*® has the answers to these questions and many more.

Learning about health can be exciting and fun. As you learn about health, you learn about yourself. Turn this page and begin to explore the world of good health.

Areas of Health

Mental Health

Family and Social Health

Growth and Development

Nutrition

Exercise and Fitness

Drugs

Diseases and Disorders

Consumer and Personal Health

Safety and First Aid

Community and Environmental Health

Table of Contents

Mental Health

Did you know . . .

▶ liking yourself helps you stay healthy?

▶ changes occur in your body when situations bother you?

Your Health and Self-Concept

Mental health is a part of your health. For good health, you need to work on having good mental health. Spend time with friends and in activities that will help you feel good about yourself.

Chapter 1

*   *describe ways to stay healthy, express feelings, and have a good self-concept.*
*   *use the responsible decision-making model and refusal skills, and make a health behavior contract.*

Kristen has a new bike. She has wanted a bike for a long time. She has promised her parents that she will take good care of it. She will follow safety rules when she rides her bike.

Knowing Yourself

Kristen's bike is important to her. When something is important to you, you take good care of it. What do you have that is important to you? How do you take care of it?

You are very important. There is only one person like you in the whole world. You need to take care of yourself.

FIGURE 1–1.
Swimming is a good
way to help you take
care of your body.

1:1 Your Health

In order to care for yourself, you should learn about health. **Health** is the condition of your mind and body and how you get along with others. Something is healthful when it is good for your mind and body. Something is healthful when it helps you get along with others.

There are three kinds of health. Physical (FIHZ ih kul) health is how your body works. Taking care of your body will help your body work as it should. Getting enough sleep and exercise helps keep your body healthy.

When do you have good mental health?

Mental health is the way you feel about yourself, and how able you are to think clearly and make wise choices. When you have good mental health, you act in ways that show you feel good about yourself. Eating healthful snacks is one way to show you make wise choices. Making wise choices shows you think clearly.

Social health is how you are able to get along with others. It includes knowing how to make and keep friends. Getting along with your family is a part of good social health. Getting along with others helps you have good physical and mental health.

1:2   Your Feelings

An important part of good health is learning to show feelings in healthful ways. Everyone has feelings. Feelings are the ways you think and feel inside. You have feelings about everything that happens to you. You can show your feelings in healthful ways.

What are feelings?

You might be sad when a friend moves away. Writing a note to your friend can help show your feelings in a healthful way. You may be happy when your team wins a soccer game. You may smile and jump for joy to show your happiness.

FIGURE 1–2. For good health, show your feelings in healthful ways.

FIGURE 1–3. Your self-concept is the way you feel about yourself.

You have many feelings. To help you know how to share your feelings in a healthful way, you may ask yourself

- What am I feeling?
- Why do I feel this way?
- How might I show this feeling in a healthful way?

Suppose a classmate pushes you while you are standing in line. You are angry. You do not think your classmate should have pushed you. You could choose to push back. You could tell your classmate how you feel. Which action is more healthful? Why should you choose this action?

1:3 Your Self-Concept

What is a healthful behavior?

Your **self-concept** (KAHN sept) is the way you feel about yourself. When you have a good self-concept you like yourself. You choose healthful behaviors. A **healthful behavior** is an action that is healthful for you and others. Eating breakfast every day is a healthful behavior. Giving a friend an apple for a snack is also healthful.

Someone with a poor self-concept might choose harmful behaviors. A person with a poor self-concept might have trouble getting along with others. This person might fight with friends often. A person with a poor self-concept might not make friends easily.

There are ways you can improve your self-concept. You can choose healthful behaviors at all times. You can try to learn new skills. You can practice skills you already have. You can be kind to your family and friends. You can obey your parents. As you work to improve the way you feel about yourself, you improve your self-concept.

ACTIVITY

About Me

Make a collage (koh LAHJ) called "About Me." A collage is a group of pictures pasted on a large board or sheet of paper. Use pictures from magazines that show healthful behaviors you would choose.

1. How does sharing with a friend help keep you healthy?
2. What are three questions you might ask yourself to know how to share your feelings?
3. How might you improve your self-concept?

Think About It

Caring About Yourself

There are ways you can show that you care about yourself. When someone asks you to do something harmful or unsafe, you can say NO. You can make and follow a plan to practice healthful behaviors. You can make responsible decisions.

1:4 Responsible Decisions ____

What is a responsible decision?

A decision is a choice you make about an action you are going to take. You make many decisions each day. A **responsible decision** is a choice that helps you have good health. Responsible decisions help you have a good self-concept.

FIGURE 1–4. Making responsible decisions helps you have good health.

10

FIGURE 1–5. Think about possible results of your decisions.

The **responsible decision-making model** is a list of steps you can use to make choices that lead to good health. Look at the steps below.

1. Describe the situation.
2. List the different decisions you may make.
3. Think about the possible results of each decision. A responsible decision is one that
   - is healthful.
   - is safe.
   - obeys the law.
   - respects self and others.
   - follows parents' or guardian's guidelines.
4. Make a responsible decision.
5. Check to see if your decision resulted in a healthful action.

How can you decide if you are making a responsible decision?

1:5 Refusal Skills _____

Sometimes, making a responsible decision means saying NO to behaviors or situations that could be harmful. Suppose a friend asks you to ride to the park on your bike. To get to the park, you must ride on a busy street. This action is not safe. Your parents do not want you to ride your bike on a busy street.

When you say NO to harmful behaviors or situations, you feel good about yourself. You improve your self-concept. You can learn to say NO. **Refusal skills** are ways you can say NO to behaviors or situations that are harmful for you and others. Here are some refusal skills you may use.

What are refusal skills?

Table 1–1

Refusal Skills
• Look directly at the person.
• Say NO clearly and firmly. "No, I do not want to ride my bike to the park."
• Give a reason for your decision. "It is not safe."
• Show you mean what you say. Move away from your bike.
• Do not change your mind.
• Tell a grown-up you trust if someone asks you to do something that is against the law.

FIGURE 1–6. A health behavior contract helps you practice a life skill and reach a goal.

1:6   A Health Behavior Contract

Life skills are healthful behaviors to learn and to practice all your life. A **health behavior contract** is a written plan that helps you practice a life skill. This plan helps you change your behavior to reach a goal. A **goal** is something toward which you work. You can set goals to have good health.

What is a goal?

Look at the health behavior contract on page 14. The goal of this health behavior contract is to exercise for good health. The life skill is to exercise at least four days each week. The plan lists ways to get exercise each day for one week.

Table 1−2

Health Behavior Contract

GOAL: _____ I will exercise for good health. _____

LIFE SKILL: _____ I will exercise four days each week. _____

MY PLAN: _____ I will make a list of exercises I enjoy. _____

1. gymnastics	3. swimming	5. shooting baskets
2. biking	4. playing soccer	6. jumping rope

The best times for me to exercise are _____ after school and on weekends. _____

HOW I FOLLOWED MY PLAN:

Day	Kind of Exercise	Amount of Time
Monday	biking	35 minutes
Tuesday	swimming	30 minutes
Wednesday		
Thursday	gymnastics	60 minutes
Friday		
Saturday	jumping rope	30 minutes
Sunday		

HOW MY PLAN WORKED: _____ I followed my plan. I feel good about _____ myself when I exercise. _____

On the health behavior contract there is a place to record how you followed your plan. There is a place to write how well your plan worked for you. Using a health behavior contract to reach a goal helps you practice a healthful behavior. It will help you improve your self-concept.

Making a plan to reach a goal is an important way to improve your health. At the end of each chapter in this textbook, you will find a list of life skills. You can use a health behavior contract to practice a life skill. Following life skills can improve your way of life. It can help you stay healthy. You can be responsible for improving your health. When you work to improve your health you will feel good about yourself.

Think About It

4. How might you know whether or not a decision is responsible?
5. When would you use refusal skills?
6. What might you do if you want to practice a life skill?

Life Skills

▶ Show your feelings in healthful ways.
▶ Try new skills and practice skills you already have to improve your self-concept.
▶ Use the responsible decision-making model when you have to make a decision.
▶ Use refusal skills to say NO to behaviors or situations that are harmful to you and others.
▶ Use a health behavior contract to practice a life skill.

Chapter 1 Review

Summary

1. There are three kinds of health. *1:1*
2. An important part of good mental health is showing feelings in healthful ways. *1:2*
3. When you have a good self-concept, you choose healthful behaviors. *1:3*
4. Using the responsible decision-making model to make wise decisions improves self-concept. *1:4*
5. When you say NO to harmful behaviors you feel good about yourself. *1:5*
6. You can practice life skills by making a health behavior contract. *1:6*

Words for Health

Complete each sentence with the correct word.
DO NOT WRITE IN THIS BOOK.

goal
health
health behavior contract
healthful behavior
life skills

refusal skills
responsible decision
responsible decison-
    making model
self-concept

1. ___ is the condition of your mind and body and how you get along with others.
2. The ___ is a list of steps you can use to make responsible decisions.
3. ___ are healthful behaviors to learn and practice for life.
4. ___ is the way you feel about yourself.
5. A ___ is an action that is healthful for you and others.

6. ___ are ways to say NO to behaviors or situations that are harmful to you and others.
7. A ___ is something toward which you work.
8. A written plan that helps you practice a life skill is a ___.

1. What are the three kinds of health?
2. How can you show your feelings in healthful ways?
3. What are three ways to improve self-concept?
4. What are the five steps in the responsible decision-making model?
5. What are four refusal skills?
6. What are the parts of a health behavior contract?

Use the life skills from this chapter to respond to the following questions.

Situation: Your friend does not do his best work in school. He does not follow classroom rules.

1. What behaviors show that your friend has a poor self-concept?
2. How can your friend feel better about himself?

Make a list of classroom manners. How would these manners improve social health?

Stress and You

David and Carlos are excited. They are about to play in a soccer game. How do you think each of them feels? What do you think is happening to their bodies?

Chapter 2

STUDENT OBJECTIVES: You will be able to

- *describe changes in the body that occur as a result of stress.*
- *make a plan to control the effects of stress.*

Some stress is a normal part of life. How will you know if stress is healthful? What will you do about stress that is harmful?

Understanding Stress

David and Carlos feel stress. Both boys feel the stress of wanting to win the game. Both boys want to run very fast. They want to kick the ball hard and play well. Understanding stress will help David and Carlos stay healthy.

2:1   What Is Stress?

Stress is the response to any demand on your mind and body. Everyone feels stress. There may be stress in your life each day. Suppose you have to sing in front of your schoolmates. You may worry that you will not sing well. You may feel stress.

What is stress?

There are causes for the stress you feel. Suppose the room you are in is very noisy. When you try to read, the noise bothers you. Noise can cause you to feel stress. Last night you may not have slept well. Being tired can cause you to feel stress. You may have a cold. Your body works hard to kill the germs that make you sick. Being sick is a cause of stress.

2:2 Your Body and Stress——

What happens to your heart when you feel stress?

Your body changes when you feel stress. Your heart beats faster than usual. It pumps blood quickly through your body. You breathe faster than usual because you need more oxygen. Sugar stored in your body goes into your blood. This sugar will give you more energy. Your mouth may become dry. Your hands may feel sweaty. Your muscles may feel tight. When have you felt this way?

FIGURE 2-1. Being sick can cause you to feel stress.

FIGURE 2–2.
Healthful stress may
help people perform at
their best.

2:3 When Stress Is Healthful ⎯

Your body's response to stress can be
healthful. **Healthful stress** is stress that causes
body changes that help you perform well.

*What is healthful
stress?*

Remember David and Carlos? Their hearts
began to beat faster because of stress. They
began to breathe faster. More sugar moved
into their blood. Both boys had extra energy.

These body changes helped each boy
during the game. After the game, the boys'
bodies returned to normal. There was not as
much sugar in their blood. The sugar was
used for energy during the game. Their
hearts were beating more slowly. Each boy
took fewer breaths because less oxygen was
needed. Their bodies were the same as
before they felt the stress of the game.

1. What are some causes of stress?
2. Why do you breathe faster when you feel
   stress?
3. How might stress be healthful?

Think About It

Controlling Stress

It is important to know the difference between healthful and harmful stress. Healthful stress helps you perform well. Harmful stress makes it hard for you to perform well. Harmful stress can make you ill. You can do something about harmful stress.

2:4   When Stress Is Harmful ___

What is harmful stress?

Harmful stress is stress that causes changes in the body that can harm health. Some changes caused by harmful stress are listed in Table 2−1.

Table 2−1

Changes Caused by Harmful Stress
Mental Changes
• You feel nervous.
• You are unable to think clearly. You worry.
• You may be unable to sleep.
Physical Changes
• Your heart works harder for a long time. This could harm your heart.
• You may feel tired all of the time.
• Your body may not be able to fight germs as easily.

Your body's response to stress is harmful when it keeps you from being able to perform well. Suppose you are going to be in a school play. You have not practiced what you need to remember to say. You worry about what will happen when it is your turn to speak in the play. You are not able to sleep. You are tired. You feel harmful stress. Stress can make you ill when it continues for a long time. Knowing what to say in the play may change the harmful stress to healthful stress.

ACTIVITY

Stress Diary

Make a chart like the one shown. Think about times you have felt stress. Were you able to perform well? How did you feel? Decide if the stress was healthful or harmful. Write about these times.

Times I Have Felt Stress

Healthful Stress	Harmful Stress
soccer game	did not begin school project on time

2:5 How to Control Stress ———

You may feel stress many times each day. Here are some ways you can limit the harmful changes caused by stress.

- Talk to your parents. They can help you find the cause of stress. Talk to your teacher or another grown-up you trust.
- Talk with friends about difficult times. Do not hide your feelings.
- Write a plan for your day and check off what you complete. Planning ahead can help you feel good about yourself.
- Exercise each day. Eat healthful foods. Get enough rest and sleep. Taking care of your body can help you respond to stress in a healthful way.

Think About It

4. How do you know when stress is harmful?
5. What are some ways you can limit harmful changes caused by stress?

Life Skills

▶ Talk to your parents and other trusted adults about any stress you feel.
▶ Plan your time wisely.
▶ Exercise, eat healthful foods, and get rest and sleep.

Health Highlights

Stress and Nutrition

During times of stress, your heart works harder than usual. If your heart and blood vessels are healthy, your body will be better able to handle stress. Food can play an important role in helping to limit harmful changes that may be caused by stress. You can make changes in your diet to keep your heart and blood vessels healthy.

Limit the amount of caffeine you eat or drink. Caffeine is a drug that makes your heart beat faster than it should. It causes you to stay awake when you need sleep. Did you know that caffeine is found in hot chocolate, chocolate candies, and some soft drinks and coffee?

Limit the amount of salt you add to food. Cut down on salty foods such as pretzels and potato chips. Too much salt may increase blood pressure.

Limit the amount of fatty foods you eat. Cut down on fried foods and red meat. Eating too many fatty foods can cause fat to stick to your artery walls. This causes your arteries to get clogged and your blood pressure to increase. Then your heart will have to work hard even when you do not feel stress.

Chapter 2 Review

Summary

1. There are many causes of stress. *2:1*
2. Your heart beats faster and you breathe more rapidly when you feel stress. *2:2*
3. Stress is healthful when body changes help you perform well. *2:3*
4. Stress is harmful when body changes cause you to perform poorly or become ill. *2:4*
5. You can limit harmful changes caused by stress. *2:5*

Words for Health

Complete each sentence with the correct word.
DO NOT WRITE IN THIS BOOK.

harmful stress   healthful stress   stress

1. ____ is the response to any demand on your mind or body.
2. ____ is stress that causes body changes that help you perform well.
3. Stress that causes body changes that can harm health is called ____.

Reviewing Health

1. What are some causes of stress?
2. What body changes do you notice when you feel stress?
3. How does the heart react to stress?
4. What are some changes caused by harmful stress?
5. Who might help you find the cause of harmful stress?

Use the life skills from this chapter to respond to the following questions.

Situation: You have a math test tomorrow. You have not had time to review or prepare for the test. You are worried you will not know how to work the problems on the test. You feel stress.

1. What kind of stress do you feel?
2. How might you control the stress you feel?
3. Why is it important to do something about stress that is harmful?

Situation: Your pet is very sick. Tomorrow, your parent has an appointment to take your pet to the vet. Your pet might need to have an operation. You are worried and unable to sleep.

1. What do you feel?
2. What are some ways you can control your stress?
3. Whom would you talk to about your problem?

1. Interview one of your favorite grown-ups. Ask this person what happens to him or her when harmful stress is felt. Ask what he or she does to help control harmful stress.
2. Talk to at least three grown-ups. Ask them to tell you about what causes them to feel stress. Make a list of these causes. Take this list to school. Work with other students to make a graph that shows what causes stress for many grown-ups.

Family and Social Health

Did you know . . .

▶ families are alike and different?

▶ following rules helps you get along with others?

Getting Along with Others

These people are enjoying an afternoon at the zoo. They are spending time with their families and friends. Family and friends are important for good health.

Chapter 3

STUDENT OBJECTIVES: You will be able to

- *tell ways to be a loving and responsible family member.*
- *make responsible decisions with friends and get along with friends and others.*

People enjoy spending time with their families. Family members enjoy each other and their friends. Getting along with family, friends, and others is important for good health.

You and Your Family

You belong to a family. Your family helps you stay healthy and safe. How does your family help keep you healthy? What does your family do to help keep you safe?

3:1 What Is a Family?

Your **family** is the group of people to whom you are related. Family members love and care about each other. A family shares work and enjoys time at play. A family shares happy times and sad times.

FIGURE 3–1.
Spending time with your family is important.

How are families different?

There are different kinds of families. Some families have no children. Many families have a mother, father, brothers, and sisters who live in the same house. Sometimes, a grandparent or other family member lives there also. Sometimes, children live with a grandparent. Some children live with other adults who care for them.

Sometimes families change. Parents may separate or become divorced. Parents who are divorced do not live with each other any more. The children may live with either the mother or father. They may visit their other parent.

If a parent remarries, then the new husband or wife becomes a stepfather or stepmother. Children in the family may have new stepbrothers or stepsisters. It takes time to learn to love and care for new family members.

32

3:2 Getting Along with Your Family

Do you get along well with everyone in your family? Getting along with your family is important. Getting along with family members is a part of good health.

One way to get along with your family is to be respectful. To be **respectful** is to show others you think what they say and do is important. Listening to what other family members say shows that you are respectful of them. It shows that you think they are important. How else can you be respectful?

What does it mean to be respectful?

Families also get along when people in the family are caring. To be **caring** is to show others love. There may be a new baby in your family. You can show love. You can help with the baby. If there are grandmothers or grandfathers in your family, you can help them with chores. If they live far away, you can write letters or talk to them on the phone.

FIGURE 3–2. Show others in your family that you care.

Families can also get along when everyone cooperates (koh AHP uh raytz). To **cooperate** is to be willing to work together with others. Family members enjoy being with each other when everyone works together. You can cooperate with someone in your family to get a job done. You can agree to work with someone in your family to solve any problems.

Families can also get along when everyone is understanding. To be **understanding** is to care how others feel. Suppose some family member is ill. Other family members need to be understanding. They can find ways to help the family member who is ill. They can also do extra work to help the family.

Some family members may have special needs. They may not hear well. They may walk with a cane or be in a wheelchair. Other family members will need to be understanding and help meet these needs.

What does it mean to be understanding?

FIGURE 3-3. Be understanding with family members.

FIGURE 3–4. A sitter may care for you when your parents are away.

3:3 Responsible Family Members

All family members need to be responsible. To be **responsible** is to act in ways that show others they can depend on you. Your parents act in responsible ways. They provide you with food. They buy you clothes. You can depend on them. They show you what it means to be responsible.

Your parents expect you to be responsible in many different situations. When you are responsible, your family knows you will do the right thing. They trust your behavior and decisions.

Everyone in a family has chores to do. Do you make your bed every day? Do you set the table at mealtime? When you are responsible, you do what is expected of you.

Sometimes your parents ask a sitter to care for you. Your parents expect the sitter to be a responsible person. They also expect good behavior from you.

What do your parents expect from you when you are with a sitter?

Think of five chores you could do to help at home. Use colored paper, scissors, and markers to make five coupons to give to your family. Write one chore on each coupon. Give these coupons to family members to use. Tell them to return the coupon to you when they need you to do that chore.

3:4   Health and Your Family ____

Your family helps you stay healthy and safe. Your parents may make sure you eat a healthful breakfast each morning. They may remind you to wear a safety belt in the car.

What is a rule?

Your parents have rules about health and safety. A **rule** is a guideline for you and others to follow. Your parents may have a rule that no one smokes in your home. If your parents do not smoke, they may ask others not to smoke in your home. The rule helps you keep your lungs healthy.

Your parents may have rules about safety for the home. They may ask that no toys be left where people walk. If you follow this rule, you or others will not trip on a toy and fall. You will stay safe. Another rule may be not to play with matches. When you follow this rule you will not cause a fire.

Your parents teach you about laws to help keep you healthy and safe. A **law** is a rule that tells you and others in your community (kuh MYEW nut ee) how to act. Your **community** is the place where you live. There is a law that says you should ride your bike in the direction of traffic. There is another law that says you are to cross the street at a crosswalk. Your parents want you to know and follow these laws. Understanding laws helps you make responsible decisions. What other laws have your parents helped you learn?

Your family has other ways to be safe and healthy. One way is to keep important phone numbers close to the telephone. Your family might list phone numbers for the fire and police departments, the Poison Control Center, and your family doctor. What other numbers might be kept close by the phone?

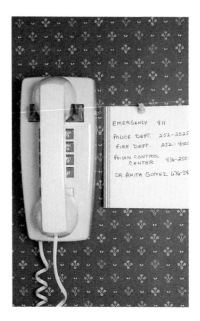

FIGURE 3–5. Keep important phone numbers close to the telephone.

1. What feelings might family members have for each other?
2. How might you show that you are respectful of other family members?
3. Why is it important to show responsible behavior when you are being cared for by a sitter?
4. Why do parents have rules for their children to follow?

Think About It

FIGURE 3–6. You have fun with friends.

You and Others

Besides family members, there are others whose company you enjoy . You enjoy the company of friends. You enjoy being with adults who are at your school and in your community. These people can help you stay healthy.

3:5 Your Friends Are Important

What is a friend?

A friend is someone you know well and like. Having a friend is important. You and a friend can have fun together no matter what you do. You can ride bikes or play games. You can do a school project together. You can enjoy spending quiet time with a friend or helping a friend.

A friend is someone with whom you can talk. You can share what you are thinking. You can share your feelings. A friend will listen to you.

There are many ways you can be a good friend. One way is to use good manners. Say "please" and "thank you." Take turns being first. Consider your friend's feelings. Say you are sorry when you are wrong or hurtful. Find ways to show your friend that you care.

How can you be a good friend?

You can have more than one friend. The friends you choose may be different. You may have a friend who enjoys the same games you enjoy. You may have another friend who enjoys the same hobby as you enjoy. You may have some friends who are boys and some who are girls. Friends may be your age. They may be older or younger than you. Older people enjoy having friends your age.

FIGURE 3–7. You can do many things with friends.

39

You may make a new friend. Perhaps a child will move into your neighborhood. Or, there may be a new student in your classroom. Think of something to do or share with this new person. Include this new person when you play with others.

3:6 Making Decisions with Friends

Choose your friends carefully. You will want to choose friends who make responsible decisions. What kinds of decisions should you make with friends?

- Decisions with friends should be healthful.
- Decisons with friends should be safe.
- Decisions with friends should follow the rules of your family.
- Decisions with friends should follow school rules and laws.
- Decisions with friends should show you care about yourself and others.

FIGURE 3–8. Choose friends who make responsible decisions.

Healthful and Safe Decisions

You and a friend can make healthful and safe decisions. Suppose you are playing ball. The ball goes into the street. You decide not to run and get the ball. You look for cars and wait until it is safe to go into the street. You make a safe decision. After playing, you are thirsty. You make a healthful decision and choose to drink fruit juice instead of a soft drink.

Family Rules, Laws, and Decisions

You and a friend go to the park to play. You take your lunches. There is a law against leaving trash on the ground. After you eat, you throw your trash in the trash can. You obey the law. You play until four o'clock. This is the time your parents want you to come home. You follow the rules of your family. Your friend also follows family rules.

Decisions That Show You Care

Your friend needs your help with some math problems. You say you will come over soon. After your friend calls, another friend invites you to play softball. You would rather play softball. You say no because you have already made plans. You show the first friend that you care. You do what you say you will do. You try not to hurt the feelings of either friend.

FIGURE 3–9. Make healthful and safe decisions with friends.

How can you show a friend that you care?

3:7 Getting Along with People

Remember the ways you learned to get along with family members. You can use the same guidelines to get along with others.

- Be respectful and caring. Let others know you think they are important.
- Be understanding and willing to cooperate.
- Act in a responsible way. Behave in ways that show others they can depend on you.
- Use good manners and consider other people's feelings.

Think About It

5. How can you be a good friend?
6. What decisions might you make with a friend to stay safe?
7. With whom is it important for you to get along?

Life Skills

- ▶ Follow family rules and community laws.
- ▶ Use skills to get along with family members and friends.
- ▶ Make decisions with friends that are healthful, safe, legal, and follow parents' rules.
- ▶ Make decisions that show you care about yourself and others.

Health Highlights

School Nurse

Susie Kranstruber is a school nurse. She enjoys the children at her school. Before school begins each year, Susie reads the school health record for each child. The school health record lists important facts about a child's health. The health record will list the shots that a child has had. Any special health problems are also listed.

Susie does screening tests. Screening tests are tests used to find changes in health. She may screen for sight and hearing. She may screen for head lice. Head lice are small insects the size of a pinhead. The signs of head lice are red spots and itching on the scalp. Children get head lice from using an infected person's comb or brush.

There are other times when a child feels ill at school. A child may have a headache or a stomachache. The child goes to Susie's room.

Sometimes Susie must help with first aid. First aid is quick treatment for injury or sudden illness. A child at school might fall on the playground. Susie may need to clean a cut or scrape and put a bandage on it. When a child has a serious injury, Susie calls the parents.

Someday you may want to be a school nurse. A school nurse can be a man or a woman. To be a school nurse you need to study many science courses. You will need to learn how to care for people. You will need to learn about many illnesses and injuries.

Chapter 3 Review

Summary

1. There are many different kinds of families. *3:1*
2. Being respectful and understanding helps you get along with your family. *3:2*
3. When you are responsible, others can count on you. *3:3*
4. Your family teaches you to be healthy and safe. *3:4*
5. It is important to have friends and to be a friend. *3:5*
6. Decisions with friends should be healthful, safe, legal, show you care about others, and follow parents' rules. *3:6*
7. There are guidelines to help you get along with people. *3:7*

Words for Health

Complete each sentence with the correct word.
DO NOT WRITE IN THIS BOOK.

caring	family	responsible
community	law	rule
cooperate	respectful	understanding

1. To be ____ is to think others are important.
2. Your ____ is the place where you live.
3. A ____ is a rule that tells you and others how to act.
4. To be ____ is to act in ways that show others they can depend on you.
5. To be ____ is to care how others feel.
6. A ____ is a guideline for you and others to follow.

7. A ____ is the group of people to whom you are related.
8. To be _____ is to show others love.
9. To _____ is to be willing to work together with others.

1. What are two ways families may be different?
2. Why might you help with a new baby in the family?
3. What are two ways you can be a responsible family member?
4. What are two rules a family might have?
5. What are three ways to be a good friend?
6. What are five guidelines for making responsible decisions with friends?
7. What are three ways to get along well with others?

Reviewing Health

Use the life skills from this chapter to respond to the following questions.
Situation: You have many trees in your yard. Your brother is raking the leaves. He asks you to help him.
1. What are some reasons for helping your brother?
2. Why should families share work?

Using Life Skills

On a sheet of paper, list five friends you have who are different ages. Write a page about why friends of all ages are important.

Extending Health

Growth and Development

Did you know . . .

▷ muscles and bones work together to help you move?

▷ you have many different body systems that are important to your health?

How Your Body Works

As you get older, you change in many ways. You learn new things and develop new interests. Your body changes too. One way your body changes is by growing. How have you changed?

Chapter 4

STUDENT OBJECTIVES: *You will be able to*

- *tell how cells, tissues, organs, and systems work together.*
- *keep muscles and bones healthy.*

Living things are alike in many ways. All living things need food, water, and air. All living things grow and change. Your body is growing and changing.

Inside Your Body

Your body is like a machine. It is made of many different parts that work together. Each part is important. Each part needs to work well for your body to be healthy.

4:1 Cells

Each of your body parts is made of cells. A **cell** is the smallest living part of a person's body. Most cells are so small they can be seen only with a microscope.

What is a cell?

Your body has many types of cells. Some types include skin cells, blood cells, muscle cells, and bone cells. Each type of cell does a special kind of work.

Your body has millions of cells. The size and shape of the cells may be different. Cells may be round, long, thin, rough, or smooth. Cells are different because they do different jobs in the body.

Why are cells different?

Your body makes new cells every day. New cells are important for your growth. Cells divide to make new cells. New cells take the place of cells that die. You grow because your body makes new cells faster than old cells die.

FIGURE 4–1. Types of body cells.

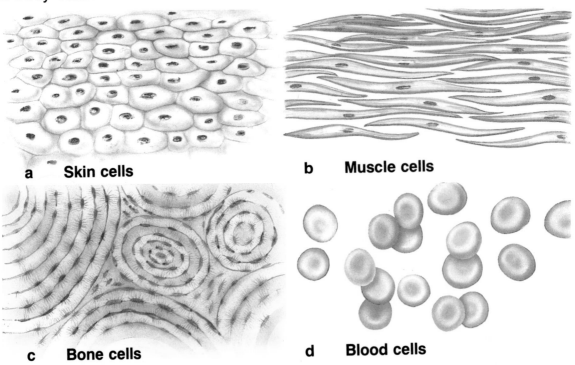

a **Skin cells**

b **Muscle cells**

c **Bone cells**

d **Blood cells**

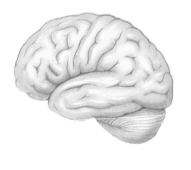

a   Brain

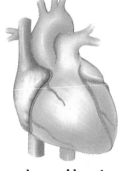

b   Heart

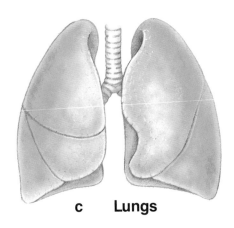

c   Lungs

FIGURE 4–2. Each organ in the body does a certain job.

4:2   Tissues, Organs, and Systems

Some cells in the body are alike. Cells that are alike form tissues (TIHSH ewz). A **tissue** is a group of cells that do the same kind of work. Muscle is an example of a tissue. Muscle is made of cells that are alike.

An **organ** is a group of tissues that work together to do a certain job. Your heart is an organ. It is made of tissues that work together to pump blood throughout your body. Your eyes and ears are also organs.

A **system** is a group of organs that work together to do a certain job. Your heart, blood, and blood vessels form a body system that helps blood travel to all cells in your body.

What is an organ?

1. How are cells different?
2. How are tissues, organs, and body systems alike?

Think About It

Bones and Muscles

Your bones and muscles make up a special team. Bones and muscles work together to help your body move.

4:3 Your Skeletal System

One of your body systems is the skeletal (SKEL ut ul) system. The **skeletal system** is the group of bones in your body. Your skeletal system gives your body support and shape.

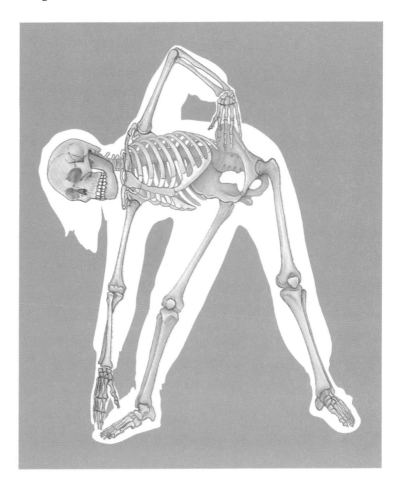

FIGURE 4–3. The skeletal system

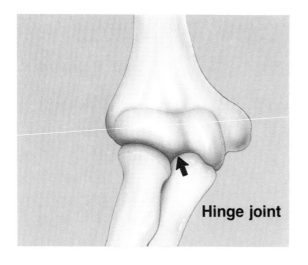

Hinge joint

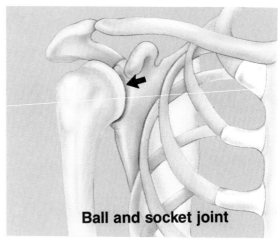

Ball and socket joint

Bones also protect your body. Your skull covers and protects your brain. Your ribs cover and protect your heart and lungs.

Bones come together or meet at different points in your body. Bones in your arm meet at your elbow. Bones in your leg meet at your knee. A **joint** is the place where bones meet.

Joints help you move in different ways. The joint at your knee helps you bend your leg. The joint at your shoulder helps you swing your arm.

4:4 Keeping Your Bones Healthy

Your bones are a very important part of you. They help you sit, walk, and stand. Exercise helps to keep bones healthy. Eating healthful foods helps keep bones strong. Foods like milk and cheese contain calcium. Calcium builds strong bones.

FIGURE 4–4. Joints help you move in different ways.

How do joints help you?

4:5 Your Muscular System ____

Your **muscular** (MUS kyuh lur) **system** is the body system made up of all the muscles in your body. Muscles help give your body shape. Some muscles are attached to bones. These muscles work with bones to help you move your body.

Muscles that help you move work in pairs. Suppose you want to kick a ball. The muscle pairs in your leg would need to move. When you move your leg back to kick, the muscle in the back of your upper leg shortens. The muscle in the front of your upper leg lengthens. When you move your leg forward, the muscle in the front of your upper leg shortens. The muscle in the back of your upper leg lengthens. Can you feel how these muscles work?

4:6 Keeping Muscles Healthy __

A machine may have many moving parts. The moving parts of a machine need care so that the machine will work well. Your muscles are like the moving parts of a machine. They need care.

You need to keep your muscular system healthy. Getting regular exercise is an important way to care for muscles. Regular exercise keeps muscles strong. Your muscles also need rest. Too much exercise and hard work can harm muscles. The right amount of exercise and rest can keep them healthy.

FIGURE 4–5.
Muscles work in pairs to help you move.

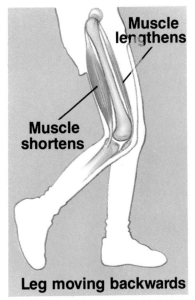

Muscle lengthens

Muscle shortens

Leg moving backwards

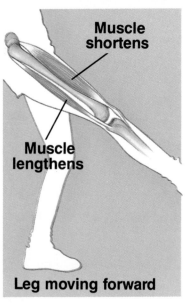

Muscle shortens

Muscle lengthens

Leg moving forward

ACTIVITY

Muscle Pairs

Make two rectangles out of heavy cardboard. Make one of them 4 inches × 6 inches. Make the other one 2 inches × 4 inches. Attach them together 1/2 inch from the bottom of each with a paper fastener. Cut a notch 2 inches from the top on each side of each rectangle. Put a rubber band into the notches, one on each side. Put another fastener in the lower corner of the top piece of cardboard. Tuck the rubber band closest to this corner under the head of the fastener. Tell what happens when you move this model of a muscle pair.

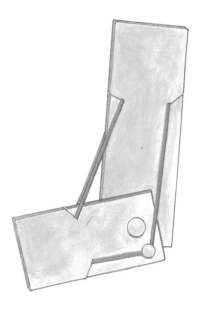

3. What is the job of your skeletal system?
4. Why is calcium important for your bones?
5. Why is exercise important to muscles?

> **Think About It**

Life Skills

▶ Eat foods with calcium to build strong bones.
▶ Exercise to help build strong bones and muscles.
▶ Get enough rest to keep your muscles healthy.

Chapter 4 Review

Summary

1. Cells have different sizes and shapes and they do different kinds of work. *4:1*
2. Your body is made of cells, tissues, and organs. *4:2*
3. Your skeletal system gives your body support. *4:3*
4. Exercise and foods with calcium help build strong bones. *4:4*
5. Muscles work in pairs to help you move. *4:5*
6. Exercise will help keep your muscles strong. *4:6*

Words for Health

Complete each sentence with the correct word.
DO NOT WRITE IN THIS BOOK.

cell	skeletal system
joint	system
muscular system	tissue
organ	

1. A group of organs that work together is a ____.
2. A ____ is a group of cells that do the same kind of work.
3. Muscles belong to the ____.
4. The smallest living part of the body is called a ____.
5. Bones belong to the ____.
6. An ____ is a group of tissues that work together.
7. The place where bones come together is a ____.

1. How are cells alike?
2. How is a tissue different from an organ?
3. What does the skeletal system do?
4. Why is eating foods with calcium important?
5. What happens when one muscle in a pair shortens?
6. How can you keep your muscles strong?

Use the life skills from this chapter to respond to the following questions.

Situation: You come home from school. You are thirsty and you want something to drink. You have a choice of a soft drink or milk.

1. Which drink would be most healthful for you?
2. Why would you make this choice?

Situation: After school you have some free time before dinner. You have a choice of playing kickball with your friends or watching TV.

1. Which activity would be the most healthful?
2. What body systems would you be helping?

Make a chart. List your favorite sports. Describe how players of each sport protect their bodies from injuries. List which body parts are protected. What do you do to protect your body when playing sports?

Body Systems and Growth

Taking good care of your body is important for good health. Work on keeping your body strong. A strong, healthy body will help you do your best.

Chapter 5

- *describe how to care for your nervous and digestive systems.*
- *describe how to keep your lungs and heart strong.*

Different body systems work together to help you grow. When you understand how these systems work, you can take better care of your body.

The Nervous and Digestive Systems

People need healthful foods to help their bodies work. Healthful foods help body actions work smoothly.

5:1 The Nervous System and Senses

Your body has a control center called the nervous (NUR vus) system. Your **nervous system** is made of organs that control all your body actions. Certain cells in these organs receive and send messages to all body parts. These messages tell your body what to do.

FIGURE 5–1. The Nervous System

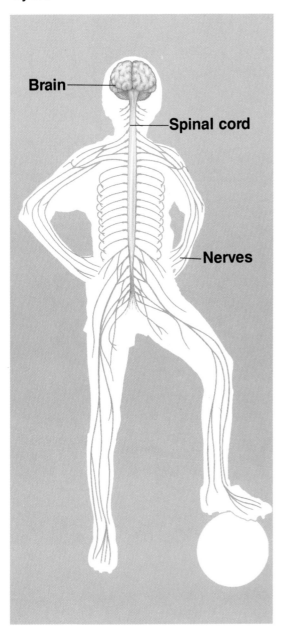

Brain

Spinal cord

Nerves

One of the most important organs in the nervous system is the brain. Your brain receives and sends messages to all your body parts. Suppose you want to catch a ball. Messages from your brain tell your eyes to follow the ball. Your brain sends messages that signal the muscles in your hands to catch the ball.

Your brain gets information from your senses. Your five senses are hearing, seeing, touching, tasting, and smelling. The sense organs—ears, eyes, skin, tongue, and nose—send messages to your brain. Your sense organs warn you of danger. They help you observe what is happening around you.

Nerve cells are cells in your body that carry messages from your sense organs to your brain. Suppose a record is playing. Nerve cells in your ear send the message to the hearing center in your brain. You hear the music. If you touch something hot, nerve cells in your skin send a message to your brain. Your brain sends a message to your muscle to pull your hand away.

Your spinal cord is another important part of your nervous system. Your spinal cord is a long strand of nerve tissue that goes from your brain down your back. It allows messages to travel between your brain and other parts of your body. Your spinal cord is surrounded by your spinal column. Your spinal column is made of bones that protect the spinal cord. The spinal column is also called the backbone.

What is the spinal cord?

You need to protect your nervous system. Protect your brain from injury by wearing a helmet when you ride a bike. Wear lap and shoulder belts in cars. These safety belts help keep your brain and spinal cord protected from injury in an accident. Avoid harmful drugs. Drugs such as alcohol and marijuana (mer uh WAHN uh) kill nerve cells. Read labels on household products. Some household products are dangerous if swallowed. They can harm your brain and nervous system.

5:2 The Digestive System

Why does your body need food?

Your body needs food for energy and growth. The **digestive** (di JES tihv) **system** is made up of organs that help your body use food. **Digestion** (di JES chun) is a process that changes the food you eat so it can be used by your body. Digestion starts in your mouth. Your teeth grind, mash, and shred food.

Saliva (suh LI vuh) is a liquid in your mouth that softens food. Small bits of food then move down a tube to your stomach. Juices in your stomach break down the food more. This food then passes into your small intestine. Digestion of food is completed in your small intestine.

FIGURE 5–3.
Digestion changes food so it can be used by your body.

Your **small intestine** is an organ that breaks down most of the food you eat into substances your body cells can use. These substances move from your small intestine into your blood. Your blood carries this food to each of your body cells.

Some food is not used by the body. This food is waste. The **large intestine** is the body organ through which solid waste passes. Muscles in the large intestine move wastes outside the body.

There are ways to keep your digestive system healthy. Eat slowly and chew your food carefully.

Foods such as fruits and vegetables help move waste through your digestive system. A bowel movement is the movement of solid wastes out of your body. Moving waste out of the body keeps your digestive system clean.

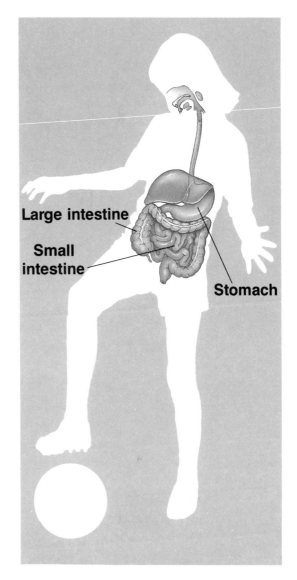

FIGURE 5–4. The Digestive System

1. How are messages carried to and from your brain and parts of your body?
2. How does saliva aid in digestion?

Think About It

FIGURE 5–5. The Circulatory System

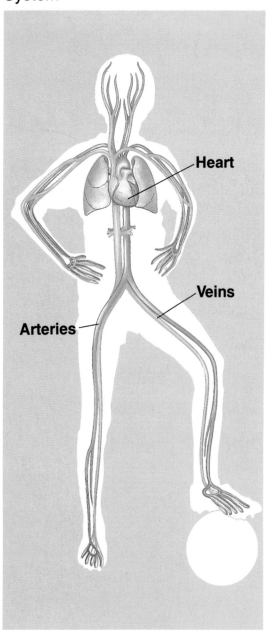

Heart

Veins

Arteries

The Circulatory and Respiratory Systems

You have body systems that provide food and oxygen to all parts of your body. These systems also carry away waste products.

5:3 The Circulatory System

The **circulatory** (SUR kyuh luh tor ee) **system** is made up of organs that move blood throughout your body. Your heart, blood, and blood vessels are all a part of your circulatory system.

Your heart pumps blood into blood vessels with each heartbeat. Blood carries substances to body cells. It carries waste products away from body cells. **Blood vessels** are tubes that carry blood. **Arteries** are blood vessels that take blood away from your heart. **Veins** are blood vessels that bring blood back to your heart.

Exercise to make your heart strong. Limit the amount of fatty foods you eat to keep your blood vessels healthy.

5:4 The Respiratory System

The **respiratory** (RES pruh tor ee) **system** is made up of organs that help you use the air you breathe. You breathe in, or inhale, air through your mouth or nose. When you inhale, the air moves through your windpipe into your lungs.

Air contains oxygen. **Oxygen** is a gas needed for you to live. Oxygen moves from your lungs into your blood. Your blood carries this oxygen to all parts of your body.

After oxygen is used by your body cells, carbon dioxide is produced. **Carbon dioxide** is a gas that is a waste product of your cells. Blood carries the carbon dioxide to your lungs. Carbon dioxide leaves your body when you breathe out, or exhale.

You can help keep your respiratory system healthy. Exercise at least three times each week. Avoid smoking and being around people who smoke. The smoke a person inhales from cigarettes can cause harm to the respiratory system.

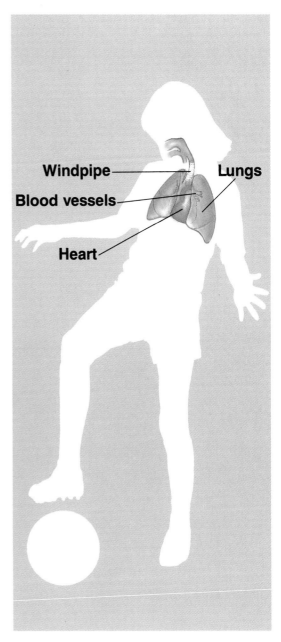

FIGURE 5–6. The Respiratory System

Windpipe

Blood vessels

Heart

Lungs

ACTIVITY

Lungs at Work

Cut off the bottom half of a plastic two-liter bottle. Using rubber bands, attach two balloons to the end of two straws. Tape the straws together. Insert the straws and balloons into the neck of the plastic bottle so that the balloons are inside. Use cotton balls to hold the straws in place. Blow into the straws and observe the air entering the "lungs." Observe what happens to the "lungs" when you stop blowing.

Think About It

3. What does your heart do?
4. How does your body rid itself of carbon dioxide?

Life Skills

▶ Wear a helmet when you ride a bike.
▶ Wear lap and shoulder belts in cars.
▶ Eat fruits and vegetables each day.
▶ Limit the amount of fatty foods you eat.
▶ Get plenty of rest and exercise.

Your Amazing Body: How It Grows

Your body systems work together to help you grow. Many changes take place in your body. You develop more bone and muscle tissue. Your bones grow longer. You get taller and heavier.

Over the next few years you will begin to grow quickly. You will get taller. You will gain weight. You will not grow at the same rate as everyone else. You will grow in your own special way. Perhaps your friends will grow faster than you. Maybe you will grow faster than your friends.

You do not control how tall you will be. Think about your mother and father. You will grow in some ways to be like them. If your mother or father is tall, then you may be tall. If both of your parents are short, you most likely will also be short.

Many changes will occur in your body over the next few years. When you become a young adult, your bones will stop growing longer. But, even when your body stops growing, it will not stop changing.

It is important to choose healthful behaviors as you grow. Eat healthful foods and get plenty of rest and exercise. This will help you grow.

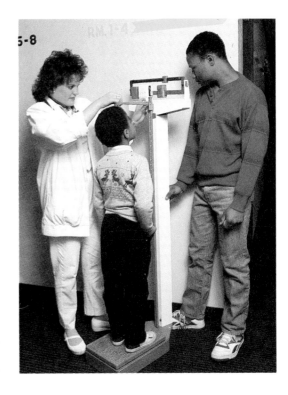

67

Chapter 5 Review

Summary

1. The nervous system controls all body actions. *5:1*

2. The digestive system helps your body use food. *5:2*

3. The heart, blood, and blood vessels move blood throughout all parts of your body. *5:3*

4. The respiratory system helps your body use oxygen and get rid of carbon dioxide. *5:4*

Words for Health

Complete each sentence with the correct word.
DO NOT WRITE IN THIS BOOK.

arteries	nervous system
blood vessels	oxygen
carbon dioxide	respiratory system
circulatory system	saliva
digestion	small intestine
digestive system	veins

1. ___ carry blood back to the heart.
2. The ___ is the body system that helps a person use food.
3. The ___ receives and sends messages to all body parts.
4. ___ softens food in the mouth.
5. ___ carry blood away from the heart.
6. The ___ helps a person breathe.

7. Blood is carried to different parts of the body in ____.

8. The process of changing food so it can be used by the body is called ____.

9. The ____ moves blood throughout the body.

10. ____ is a gas needed by the body.

11. The ____ is an organ that digests most of the food a person eats.

12. ____ is a gas that is a waste product of body cells.

1. How does the brain get information?
2. What is the job of the large intestine?
3. How do arteries and veins differ?
4. How does oxygen reach body cells?

Use the life skills from this chapter to respond to the following questions.

Situation: You want a snack. You have a choice of eating fruit or ice cream.

1. Which would be better for your digestive system?
2. Why would this be the better choice?

Draw a cartoon to show how nerve cells might send a message to the brain. Be sure to include all of the body parts needed to get information to the brain.

Nutrition

Did you know . . .

▶ you can choose foods for a healthful diet?

▶ it is healthful to limit the amount of sugar and salt you eat?

Planning a Healthful Diet

Picnics can be fun. These children are planning a picnic with their parents. They are choosing a variety of foods. Many of their choices include healthful foods.

Chapter 6

STUDENT OBJECTIVES: *You will be able to*

● *name the seven diet goals, the food groups, and ways to be at a healthful weight.*
● *make healthful diet choices.*

Eating healthful foods means making wise choices. To make wise choices, you need to know what foods are healthful. You need to learn what foods will improve your diet.

Eating Healthful Foods

It is important to make healthful choices about foods. For good health, eat a wide variety of foods each day. Following certain diet goals will help you make healthful choices.

6:1   Diet Goals

Diet goals are guidelines for eating to help you live longer and more healthfully. There are seven diet goals.

Follow these seven diet goals to help you make healthful choices.

1. Eat a variety of foods.
2. Be at a healthful weight.
3. Eat few fatty foods.
4. Eat more fiber.
5. Eat less sugar.
6. Use less salt.
7. Do not drink alcohol.

In this chapter, you will study how to choose foods that help you follow the seven diet goals.

6:2 Eat a Variety of Foods_____

What is a nutrient?

There are many different kinds of foods. Each food belongs to a food group. A food group is made up of foods that contain the same nutrients. A **nutrient** is a material in food that helps your body work as it should. Some nutrients help you grow. Some provide energy for you to run and play. **Energy** is the power that helps your body work.

FIGURE 6–1. Your body needs nutrients for energy to help you run and play.

a

b

FIGURE 6–2. You need foods from (a) the milk group and (b) the meat group each day.

There are four healthful food groups. These groups include the milk group, meat group, fruit and vegetable group, and grain group. For good health, choose foods from these four healthful food groups.

Milk Group

Milk, cheese, and yogurt are in the milk group. Milk and foods made with milk help you have strong bones and teeth. You need three servings from the milk group each day. You can drink milk or eat foods made with milk to get the daily servings you need.

Meat Group

Beef, poultry, fish, eggs, and nuts are foods in the meat group. These foods help make your muscles strong. They help your body grow. You need two servings from the meat group each day.

What foods belong to the meat group?

a

b

FIGURE 6–3. You need foods from (a) the fruit and vegetable group and (b) the grain group each day.

How many servings do you need each day from the fruit and vegetable group?

Fruit and Vegetable Group

Apples, grapes, carrots, and broccoli are examples of foods in the fruit and vegetable group. What other foods are fruits? What other foods are vegetables? Fruits and vegetables help keep your eyes, skin, and hair healthy. Fruits and vegetables also help you grow. Some foods in this group help you have healthy bones. Other foods in this group help you have healthy gums. You need four servings from the fruit and vegetable group each day.

Grain Group

Foods in the grain group come from plants. Grains include wheat, oats, rice, barley, and rye. Breads and cereals are made from grains.

Foods made from grains provide energy for your body. Some grain foods help you have daily bowel movements. You need four servings from the grain group each day.

Some foods are made up of foods from more than one food group. Suppose you are having macaroni and cheese for lunch. What are the main ingredients in macaroni and cheese? In what food group does each ingredient belong?

Macaroni and cheese is a combination food. Combination foods are made up of foods from two or more healthful food groups. Pizza, vegetable soup, and spaghetti and meatballs are combination foods. Servings of these foods can be a part of your diet. What combination foods do you like?

Some foods are not healthful to eat. These foods belong to the others group. The others group is made up of foods that have too many fats or sugars. Eating too many of these foods may cause you to gain weight. They can cause tooth decay. They are not healthful for your heart and arteries. You should make a plan to eat few foods from this group.

What are combination foods?

FIGURE 6–4.
Combination foods contain foods from more than one food group.

A snack is a food you eat between meals. You should always choose healthful snacks to eat. Make a list of your favorite snacks. Write the four healthful food groups, the combination group, and the others group at the top of a chart. List your snacks under the correct food group.

6:3 Be at a Healthful Weight

Your body works best when you are at the weight that is right for you. Your doctor can tell you if you are at a healthful weight. You may weigh too much for your height and build. Or, you may already be at a healthful weight.

You can make wise choices to help you be at a healthful weight. You can choose to eat few foods with fat or sugar. It is also important to exercise.

Think About It

1. Why should you follow the seven diet goals?
2. What are some ways nutrients help your body?
3. Why is it important to be at a healthful weight?

Diet Choices

Suppose you are at a grocery store. Your parents ask you to take a cart and fill it with healthful foods for a family meal. You want to make wise choices. You want to make choices that will help you follow the seven diet goals.

6:4   Eat Few Fatty Foods

One wise diet choice is to eat few fatty foods. Blood carries food to all parts of your body through arteries. Look at Figure 6–5. This picture shows two arteries. One artery is clear. The other has fatty material in it. For good health, you want your arteries clear. With clear arteries, your heart does not have to work as hard to pump blood. Foods that have animal fats may cause fatty material to collect in arteries.

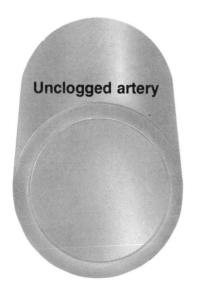
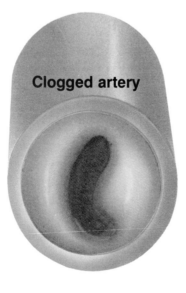

Unclogged artery   **Clogged artery**

FIGURE 6–5. Avoid fatty foods to help prevent clogged arteries.

Foods that have animal fats include hamburger, steak, and bacon. Foods cooked in animal fats also may add fatty material to your arteries. You can reduce the amount of fat you eat. Try to eat these foods less often. Limit the food you eat that is cooked in butter or margarine.

6:5   Eat More Fiber

What is fiber?

Fiber is a material in food that helps wastes move through the body. The skins of many fruits contain fiber. Leafy vegetables, such as lettuce and cabbage, have some fiber. There is fiber in whole grain breads and cereals.

Eat foods with fiber every day. Drink plenty of water. Eating foods that have fiber and drinking water will help you have regular bowel movements. Regular bowel movements will help keep your digestive system healthy.

FIGURE 6–6. You should eat foods with fiber every day.

FIGURE 6–7. Natural sugars are found in fresh fruits.

6:6   Eat Less Sugar

Some foods, like apples and oranges, have natural sugar in them. Some vegetables also have natural sugar. Natural sugar is the sugar that is in foods and has not been added. Foods with natural sugar are healthful. They give you energy.

What is natural sugar?

Sugar is added to many foods. Candy, cakes, and many soft drinks are made with added sugar. Sugar is also added to some cereals.

Your body needs some sugar. You can get enough sugar by eating fruits and vegetables. You do not need the added sugar found in other foods. Too much sugar may cause cavities. Too much sugar can cause you to gain extra weight. For good health

- eat foods with natural sugars.
- do not add sugar to fruits or cereals.
- eat few foods made with added sugars.

6:7 Use Less Salt

How much salt do you need each day?

You need less than a teaspoon of salt each day. Too much salt may cause your heart to work too hard. Salt is already in many of the foods you eat. Salt is in many breads. It is in many canned foods, such as soups and vegetables. You can get all the salt you need without adding salt to your food. For good health

- add little or no salt to food.
- do not add salt to water in which foods are cooked.
- eat few salty snacks like potato chips and pretzels.

6:8 Make Wise Food Choices at the Store

You have learned about wise diet choices. Think about these choices when you help shop for food. There are other facts you should know when choosing food.

FIGURE 6–8. Make wise food choices when you shop.

FIGURE 6-9. Read the label on foods before you buy.

Most foods have labels on them. A **food label** lists the ingredients in the food. For example, a box of cereal may have a label listing sugar, wheat, and salt. The ingredient that appears first makes up the largest part of the food. Check food labels to see how healthful the food is.

Begin checking food labels. You may learn that sugar is added to your cereal. You check the food label of another box of cereal. It has no added sugar. You may decide to buy the cereal without sugar.

As a wise shopper, you also compare the prices of foods. Suppose you see two brands of canned fruit. One brand costs less than the other. You check the food labels. Both have the same ingredients. You can buy the brand that costs less.

How can you be a wise shopper?

FIGURE 6–10. It is wise to eat healthful foods.

Think About It

4. Why should you keep your arteries clear of fat?
5. Why is it important to eat foods with fiber?
6. Why might you eat less sugar?
7. Why might you use less salt?
8. Why is it important to read food labels?

Life Skills

▶ Eat a variety of foods.
▶ Be at a healthful weight.
▶ Eat fewer fatty foods.
▶ Eat foods with fiber.
▶ Eat less sugar.
▶ Use less salt.
▶ Read food labels.
▶ Compare food prices.

Food Service Worker

Lillian Hodges works in a school cafeteria. She follows certain health rules. Before she prepares foods, Lillian washes her hands to remove germs. Then she checks to see that the dishes, spoons, and pans she will use are clean. She washes the tabletop where she will work.

Lillian washes all the fruits and vegetables. She knows they might have chemicals on them. She serves the fruit without cooking it. She either cooks the vegetables very little or not at all. Fruits and vegetables are most healthful served this way.

Lillian checks the other foods. She looks for the date stamped on the milk containers to see if the milk is fresh. She also checks meats for good color and freshness.

The lunch she serves includes foods from all the healthful food groups. She has followed the diet goals. Her meal is low in fat, sugar, and salt; it contains fiber.

After lunch, Lillian washes the dishes. She wraps and stores leftover food in the refrigerator. She also checks to see what she can do to prepare for the next school lunchtime.

Chapter 6 Review

Summary

1. There are seven diet goals for healthful eating. *6:1*
2. You need servings from the healthful food groups each day. *6:2*
3. Make wise choices to help you be at a healthful weight. *6:3*
4. Too many fatty foods may add fatty material to your arteries. *6:4*
5. Foods with fiber and water help you have regular bowel movements. *6:5*
6. Too much sugar causes cavities. *6:6*
7. Too much salt may cause the heart to work harder than usual. *6:7*
8. Food labels and prices help you make wise choices. *6:8*

Words for Health

Complete each sentence with the correct word.
DO NOT WRITE IN THIS BOOK.

diet goals   food label

energy   nutrient

fiber

1. A ___ is a material in food that helps your body work as it should.
2. A ___ lists the ingredients in the food.
3. ___ is the power that helps your body work.
4. ___ is a material in food that helps wastes move through the body.

5. The ___ are guidelines for eating to help you live longer and more healthfully.

1. What are the seven diet goals?
2. What are the four healthful food groups?
3. Who can tell you if you are at a healthful weight?
4. Why might eating too many fatty foods be harmful?
5. What are two foods that contain fiber?
6. What are two ways to eat less sugar?
7. What are two ways to eat less salt?
8. What information is found on a food label?

Use the life skills from this chapter to respond to the following questions.
Situation: One of your parents goes to the doctor. The doctor says your family should eat fewer fatty foods.
1. Why is it harmful to eat too many fatty foods?
2. What foods could your family choose that have less fat?

Write a report about a dietitian. Find out what this person does. Describe the training needed for this important health career.

Exercise and Fitness

Did you know . . .

▶ being in good physical condition keeps you from tiring easily?

▶ there are ways to stay safe when you play sports and games?

Physical Fitness and Health

Having physical fitness will help you have a healthy body. It also will help you do well in sports and games. You can make a plan to develop physical fitness.

Chapter 7

STUDENT OBJECTIVES: You will be able to

- *define physical fitness and tell ways to keep muscles in good condition.*
- *make and follow a plan for heart fitness and a low amount of body fat.*

Many boys and girls enjoy swimming. Swimming helps you have a strong, healthy body. What other activities help you to be strong and healthy? Why is it important to be strong and healthy?

Physical Fitness

You need to have good physical fitness to be healthy. Good physical fitness can help you in sports and games. You can work to improve your fitness.

7:1 What Is Physical Fitness?

Physical fitness is the condition of your body. When your body is healthy and strong, you have energy to work and play.

FIGURE 7–1. You need muscular strength for many activities.

How does physical fitness help your body?

When you have good physical fitness, your heart, lungs, and muscles are strong. Your body is firm and able to move easily. You are more likely to stay healthy. You are more likely to be at a healthful weight for you. Physical fitness is important for good health.

There are five parts of physical fitness. These parts are

- muscular strength.
- muscular endurance.
- flexibility.
- heart fitness.
- a low amount of body fat.

You can work to improve each of these five parts of fitness. When you improve your fitness, you will look and feel better. You will be able to perform better at school. When you play sports and games, you will be able to play at your best.

7:2 Muscular Strength

Strong muscles are needed for good physical fitness. Using your muscles makes them strong. **Muscular strength** is the ability of your muscles to lift, pull, and push.

Climbing a rope or doing pull-ups makes your arm muscles strong. Riding a bike or jogging makes your leg muscles strong. Muscles become weak when they are not used often.

What is muscular strength?

7:3 Muscular Endurance

Muscular endurance (ihn DOOR unts) is the ability to use your muscles for a long time. For activities like making your bed, your muscles have to work for only a short time. When you walk or run, your muscles are used over and over again. Do activities that use the same muscles many times to develop muscular endurance.

FIGURE 7–2. You need muscular strength for many activities.

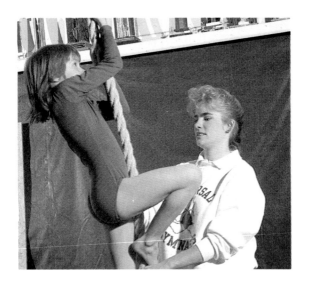

7:4 Flexibility

What is flexibility?

People stretch their muscles to develop flexibility (flek suh BIHL ut ee). **Flexibility** is the ability to bend and move easily. Stretching your muscles makes your body ready to move in many ways. It helps prevent muscle injury.

You need to stretch your muscles each day. You should stretch the muscles in your legs, arms, and waist. You should also remember to stretch your back muscles.

ACTIVITY

Stretching for Flexibility

Stand on the tips of your toes. Raise your arms over your head. Point your fingers upward. Pretend you are trying to reach the sky. Stretch as high as possible. Count to ten. Bend over at your waist. Bend your knees slightly. Slowly try to touch your toes with your fingers. Count to ten. Repeat this activity five times.

Think About It

1. How might physical fitness help you?
2. How does having strong muscles help you?
3. During what kinds of activities must you have muscular endurance?
4. How often do you need to stretch your muscles?

Your Fitness

When you are in good physical condition, you have a strong heart. Your amount of body fat is low. Having a physical fitness plan helps you reach these goals.

7:5 Heart Fitness

Your heart is a muscle. Like other muscles in your body, your heart needs physical activity to be strong. Your heart works every time it beats. With each beat, blood moves out of the heart to other parts of the body. **Heart fitness** is the condition of your heart and blood vessels. A strong heart pushes more blood out with each beat than a weak heart. Between beats, the heart rests. A strong heart is able to rest longer between beats than a weak heart.

What is heart fitness?

FIGURE 7–3.
Running helps make your heart strong.

FIGURE 7–4. You can help make your heart strong.

Many activities help make your heart strong. Swimming, running, biking, and walking are good activities for your heart. Exercise often to help keep your heart strong. Any plan to exercise should be done in the following way.

- Do activities like swimming, running, biking, or walking three to five times a week.
- Exercise slowly at first.
- Slow down your activity if breathing becomes difficult.
- You should be able to talk while you exercise.
- Have fun while you exercise.

7:6 Amount of Body Fat

Your body is made up of lean tissue and fat tissue. Lean tissue includes your muscles, bones, nerves, skin, and body organs. Fat tissue is the fat stored beneath your skin and around your body organs.

What is fat tissue?

For good physical fitness, it is best to have a high amount of lean tissue and a small amount of fat tissue. Activities that make your heart and other muscles strong help decrease your amount of fat tissue. These activities also increase your amount of lean tissue.

7:7 Testing Your Fitness

There are two tests that measure physical fitness. One test is called the President's Challenge. The other test is called Physical Best. Your physical education teacher can use one of these tests to help you measure your fitness. Look at pages 98 and 99 to see what activities are in these tests.

What are two tests that measure physical fitness?

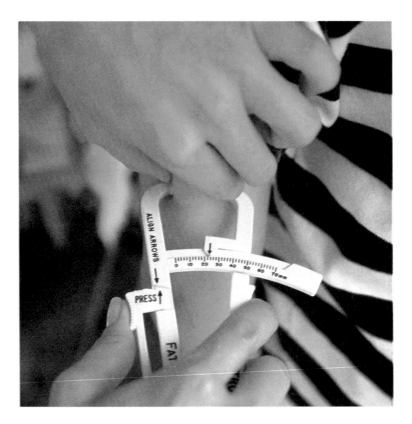

FIGURE 7–5. The amount of fat tissue is a measure of fitness.

The activities in the President's Challenge test are curl-ups, pull-ups, the v-sit reach, the one-mile walk/run, and the shuttle run. The activities in the Physical Best test are modified sit-ups, pull-ups, sit and reach, one-mile walk/run, and a measure of the amount of body fat.

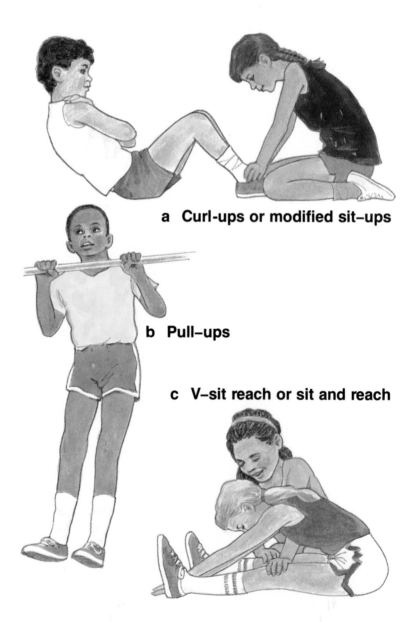

a Curl-ups or modified sit–ups

b Pull–ups

c V–sit reach or sit and reach

You may take one of these tests two times a year. After the first test, you may set goals to do better the second time you are tested.

e Shuttle run

d One–mile walk/run

f Amount of body fat

Suppose that you do not do well on your fitness test. You may find that you do not have good physical fitness. What can you do? Talk with your physical education teacher and find out what activities you can do to improve your fitness. You may use a health behavior contract to help you reach your goal.

Table 7−1

Health Behavior Contract

Goal: I will improve my fitness.

Life Skill: I will work to improve my fitness tests scores.

My Plan: I will stretch four times a week to increase my score on the v-sit reach test.

How I Followed My Plan:

Day	Kind of Activity	Number of times held ten seconds
Sunday	thigh stretch	6
Monday	toe touch	4
Tuesday	calf stretch	5
Wednesday		
Thursday	arm stretch	4
Friday		
Saturday		

How My Plan Worked: I stretched four times this week. I am improving my flexibility.

FIGURE 7–6. These badges are fitness awards.

If you pass one of the physical fitness tests, you will win an award. Look at Figure 7–6 to see the seals that appear on the fitness awards.

5. How might you develop heart fitness?
6. Which kinds of activities help keep a healthy amount of body fat?
7. How might you find out if your body is in good physical condition?

Think About It

Life Skills

▶ Exercise your muscles to have muscular strength, muscular endurance, and flexibility.

▶ Exercise often to have heart fitness and a low amount of body fat.

Chapter 7 Review

Summary

1. Physical fitness is the condition of your body. *7:1*
2. Activities for muscular strength help make muscles strong. *7:2*
3. Activities for muscular endurance help muscles work a long time. *7:3*
4. Stretching improves flexibility. *7:4*
5. Activities like swimming, running, biking, and walking help make the heart strong. *7:5*
6. Activities that make the heart stronger also decrease the amount of fat tissue. *7:6*
7. You can take tests that help check your fitness. *7:7*

Words for Health

Complete each sentence with the correct word.
DO NOT WRITE IN THIS BOOK.

flexibility   muscular strength
heart fitness   physical fitness
muscular endurance

1. ___ is the condition of your heart and blood vessels.
2. ___ is the ability to use your muscles for a long time.
3. ___ is the condition of your body.
4. ___ is the ability to bend and move easily.
5. The ability of your muscles to lift, pull, and push is ___.

1. What are five parts of physical fitness?
2. What activities help make your leg muscles strong?
3. Why do you need muscular endurance?
4. How does stretching your muscles help you?
5. How can exercising help the heart muscle?
6. What kind of activities help decrease fat tissue?
7. What can you do if your body is not in good physical condition?

Use the life skills from this chapter to respond to the following questions.

Situation: You are going on a vacation with your family to hike in the mountains. You have never done much hiking before. You have a month to prepare.

1. What kinds of activities will help you prepare?
2. How will these activities improve your physical fitness?

Situation: A friend of yours visits the doctor for a checkup. The doctor tells your friend that he has too much fat tissue.

1. Why is too much fat tissue not healthy?
2. How might your friend decrease his amount of fat tissue?

Pretend you are a coach for a soccer team. Write a one-page speech to tell your players about the importance of physical fitness.

Physical Fitness and Skills

These children are enjoying their gymnastics lesson. They are learning gymnastics and improving fitness skills. Practicing these skills will help them become good gymnasts.

Chapter 8

STUDENT OBJECTIVES: *You will be able to*

- *name fitness skills and tell why they are important for sports and games.*
- *make a plan to develop skills and stay safe in sports and games.*

Many children enjoy playing sports and games. Playing games with others is healthful. What sports and games do you enjoy?

Your Skills

Some people play sports and games better than others. These people may have learned fitness skills.

8:1 What Are Fitness Skills?___

Skills are actions that help you do something well. **Fitness skills** are actions that help you do physical activities. Having fitness skills helps you become good at sports and games. You are also less likely to get hurt. Fitness skills are discussed in the following sections.

8:2 Agility and Balance ———

Have you ever watched a basketball game? A basketball player must have agility (uh JIHL ut ee). **Agility** is the ability to change directions quickly. For what other games do you need agility?

You can test yourself to find out if you have agility. Use chalk to draw a line with several sharp turns on the sidewalk. Run forward on the line as fast as you can. Were you able to stay on the line? What did you discover about your agility?

When you run, you need balance. **Balance** is the ability to keep from falling. You need balance for many activities you do every day. You need balance to ride a bike. You need balance to do a cartwheel.

What is agility?

FIGURE 8–1. Having balance will help keep you from falling.

FIGURE 8-2. You need coordination to play many sports and games.

8:3 Coordination and Reaction Time

Remember the last time you hit a ball with a bat. Your eyes watched the ball. At just the right moment, you moved your arms and hands. You used coordination (koh ord un AY shun). **Coordination** is the ability to use more than one body part at a time. To hit the ball, you used your eyes, arms, and hands.

What is coordination?

You also used another fitness skill. As you hit the ball, nerves in your eyes sent a message to your brain. Your arms and hands began moving so you could hit the ball. You hit the ball at the right time. You had good reaction time. **Reaction time** is the amount of time it takes your muscles to respond to a message from your brain.

8:4 Speed and Power

What is speed?

Soccer players use fitness skills to play soccer. They use speed to run down the field. **Speed** is the ability to move fast. The players kick the ball with power. **Power** is the ability to use strong muscles. Power helps the players kick the ball hard. Kicking with power makes the ball go fast and far.

ACTIVITY

Testing Your Speed and Power

You will test your speed and power. Your teacher will measure a distance on the playground. See how fast you can run that distance. How much speed do you have? Your teacher will have a soccer ball. Kick the ball as hard as you can. How far did it go? Do you have much power?

Think About It

1. How can having fitness skills help you enjoy kickball?
2. How does balance help you when you play?
3. Why is reaction time important to a softball player?
4. Why does a soccer player need speed and power?

FIGURE 8–3. Parents may help you learn skills.

Fitness Skills and Safety

Think about the sports and games you enjoy. You can develop fitness skills for these activities. Developing fitness skills can help you stay safe when playing sports and games.

8:5 Developing Fitness Skills

When you play sports and games, you use different fitness skills. Many children take lessons to learn how to play a sport and improve fitness skills.

Some children take tennis lessons or swimming lessons. They practice the skills they learn. Practicing the skills helps them become better at the sport or game.

Some children play on teams. Perhaps you have played on a soccer team or a baseball team. Players need to practice skills to learn to play well as a team.

Family members, teachers, or friends may help you learn skills. If you practice what you learn, you will improve your skills.

How can you improve your fitness skills?

8:6   Safety in Sports and Games

Before you play a sport or game, take time to warm up your muscles. Exercising to warm up muscles gets them ready to do more work. If you plan to play soccer, you might stretch and run slowly. If you warm up your muscles, you may prevent injury when you play.

After you play a sport or game, take time to cool down. Exercising to cool down slows your heart rate. Exercising also stretches your muscles. You may prevent some muscle soreness.

There are other ways to stay safe when you play sports and games. Wear the right clothes, shoes, and equipment for the sport or game you are going to play. Always play in a safe place. Follow the rules for the sport or game you are playing.

Think About It

5. How might you improve fitness skills?

6. How can you stay safe when playing games?

Life Skills

▶ Practice to improve your fitness skills.

▶ Warm up before and cool down after playing.

▶ Wear the right clothing, shoes, and equipment for sports and games.

▶ Follow rules to stay safe when playing.

Health Highlights

Tennis Coach

Lucy Manifold enjoys being a tennis coach. A coach is a person who helps people develop skills to play a sport. Lucy is the coach for a high school tennis team. She helps the players learn how to improve their skills. She helps them prepare to play against other tennis players.

A coach should set a good example for his or her players. Lucy practices fitness and tennis skills. She also chooses healthful behaviors. She jogs and eats healthful foods. She warms up before and cools down after exercise. Lucy sets a good example as a coach.

Chapter 8 Review

Summary

1. Fitness skills help you become good at sports and games and help keep you from getting hurt. *8:1*

2. Agility helps you change directions quickly, and balance helps keep you from falling. *8:2*

3. Coordination allows you to use more than one body part at a time, and reaction time allows you to respond quickly. *8:3*

4. Speed and power can help you move fast and use strong muscles. *8:4*

5. Lessons and practice help you learn a sport and improve fitness skills. *8:5*

6. There are ways to stay healthy and safe when playing sports and games. *8:6*

Words for Health

Complete each sentence with the correct word.
DO NOT WRITE IN THIS BOOK.

agility   power
balance   reaction time
coordination   speed
fitness skills

1. ___ are actions that help you do physical activities.
2. ___ is the ability to move fast.
3. ___ is the ability to change directions quickly.
4. ___ is the ability to use more than one body part at a time.
5. The ability to use strong muscles is ___.

6. ___ is the amount of time it takes your muscles to respond to a message from your brain.
7. ___ is the ability to keep from falling.

1. What are ways fitness skills help you?
2. How does agility help you play games?
3. Why does a football player need coordination?
4. How does speed help you win a race?
5. Who are some people who might help you develop skills?
6. What are some ways to stay healthy and safe while playing sports and games?

Use the life skills from this chapter to respond to the following questions.
Situation: Your family is planning a bike trip. You will ride a long distance. Your family decides to work on fitness skills for the trip.
1. How are each of the fitness skills used in biking?
2. What might you do to improve your fitness skills?

1. Make a list of the places in your community where you can take lessons for sports and games.
2. Interview an athlete in your community. Find out what skills this person uses. What is this person's plan for practicing these skills?

Drugs

Did you know . . .

▷ drugs are found in medicine?

▷ drugs can be very dangerous?

▷ alcohol and tobacco are drugs?

Unit 6

Drugs Used as Medicine

Medicines can be used to help you feel better when you are ill. They can help cure some kinds of illnesses. Knowing how to correctly and safely use medicines is important.

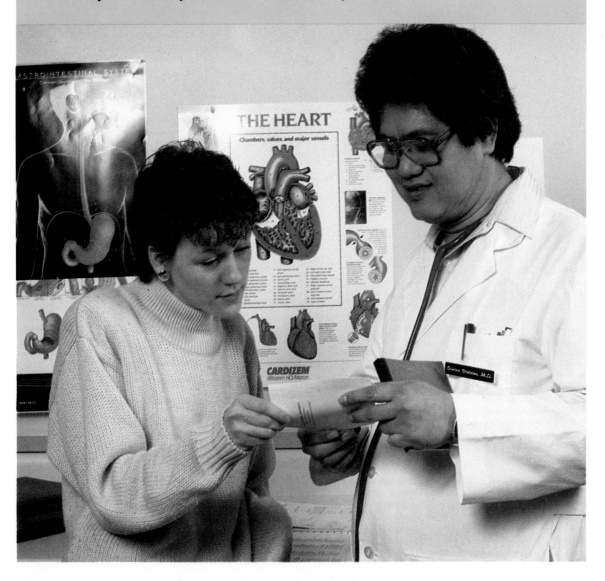

Chapter 9

At some time in your life, you probably have been given medicine. Medicine can be helpful to people of all ages. Knowing how to use medicine correctly and safely is important for everyone.

Medicines

Drugs can be important to your health. They can help keep germs from harming your body. They can help you feel better when you are ill.

9:1 What Is a Drug?

A **drug** is a chemical that changes how your body works. A drug can change the way you feel. It can also change the way you think and act.

FIGURE 9–1. When you are ill, your doctor may give you medicine.

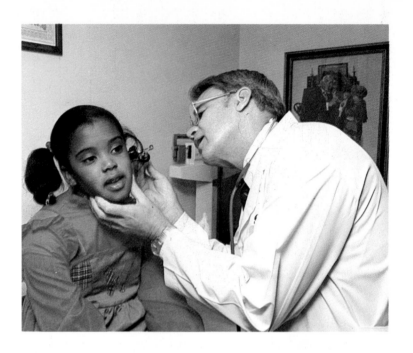

What is a medicine?

Think about the last time you were ill. Perhaps your parent gave you a medicine. A **medicine** is a drug used to treat an illness or injury. A medicine can help a sick person become well.

Medicines can help cure some kinds of illnesses. To **cure** means to make well. Suppose you have an earache caused by germs. Your doctor gives you a medicine. The medicine kills the germs. Your earache is gone and you feel better.

Suppose a person has an illness that cannot be cured. This person may need to take medicine to help certain body organs work. The medicine will help the person feel better though the illness is not cured. This person may always have to take that kind of medicine.

Some medicines get rid of symptoms (SIHM tumz) of an illness. A **symptom** is a signal that you may be sick. A cough and runny nose may be symptoms of a cold. A fever and headache may be symptoms of flu.

What is a symptom?

Medicines cannot cure a cold or flu. They can only relieve the symptoms. A medicine may stop your cough and runny nose. Although these symptoms are relieved, you still have a cold or flu. When you can relieve the symptoms of an illness, you feel better.

9:2 Over-the-Counter Drugs

Medicines that relieve symptoms can be bought at some stores. Some of these medicines are called over-the-counter drugs. **Over-the-counter** (OTC) **drugs** are drugs that can be bought without an order from a medical doctor.

FIGURE 9–2.
Medicines can help relieve symptoms of an illness.

119

FIGURE 9–3. Where can you buy over-the-counter drugs?

Aspirin and cough syrup are examples of some over-the-counter drugs. OTC drugs are sold in drugstores. These drugs may also be sold in grocery and department stores.

Over-the-counter drugs must be used in the correct way. The directions for safe use should be followed. These drugs can be harmful if you do not take them the correct way. Only a grown-up should give you an over-the-counter drug.

9:3 Prescription Drugs

Some medicines can only be bought with a prescription (prih SKRIHP shun). A **prescription** is a written order for a medicine. Medical doctors and dentists can write a prescription.

A prescription tells a pharmacist (FAR muh sust) what medicine the doctor has ordered. A **pharmacist** is a person who prepares medicine for you. He or she may work in a drugstore, hospital, or in the drug department of a large store.

A **prescription drug** is a drug ordered by a medical doctor or dentist. It is prepared for only one person. A prescription drug has a label. The label tells who is supposed to use the drug. Only that person should use the drug. The label also tells how the drug is to be used. The drug should be used only as directed. Always check with your parent before you take any medicine. Look at Figure 9–4. What doctor ordered the medicine? What is the name of the medicine? How often should it be taken?

What is a prescription drug?

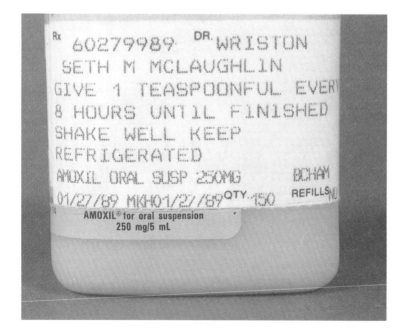

FIGURE 9–4. The label on a prescription drug tells whom it is for and how to use it.

Read the drug labels below. Which medicine is an over-the-counter drug? Which one is a prescription drug? What information is on each label? What are the names of the drugs? Write the answers to the questions on a sheet of paper.

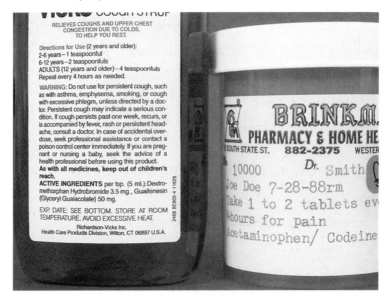

VICKS COUGH SYRUP

RELIEVES COUGHS AND UPPER CHEST
CONGESTION DUE TO COLDS,
TO HELP YOU REST.

Directions for Use (2 years and older):
2-6 years – 1 teaspoonful
6-12 years – 2 teaspoonfuls
ADULTS (12 years and older) – 4 teaspoonfuls
Repeat every 4 hours as needed.

WARNING: Do not use for persistent cough, such as with asthma, emphysema, smoking, or cough with excessive phlegm, unless directed by a doctor. Persistent cough may indicate a serious condition. If cough persists past one week, recurs, or is accompanied by fever, rash or persistent headache, consult a doctor. In case of accidental overdose, seek professional assistance or contact a poison control center immediately. If you are pregnant or nursing a baby, seek the advice of a health professional before using this product. **As with all medicines, keep out of children's reach.**
ACTIVE INGREDIENTS per tsp. (5 ml.): Dextromethorphan Hydrobromide 3.5 mg., Guaifenesin (Glyceryl Guaiacolate) 50 mg.

EXP. DATE: SEE BOTTOM. STORE AT ROOM TEMPERATURE. AVOID EXCESSIVE HEAT.
Richardson-Vicks Inc.
Health Care Products Division, Wilton, CT 06897 U.S.A.

2466 BC005-4 11626

BRINKM.
PHARMACY & HOME HE
SOUTH STATE ST.   882-2375   WESTER
10000   Dr. Smith
Joe Doe 7-28-88rm
Take 1 to 2 tablets ev
4hours for pain
Acetaminophen/ Codeine

Think About It

1. How can medicines help you if you are ill?
2. How can you use an over-the-counter drug safely?
3. Why should you never take another person's prescription drug?

FIGURE 9–5. Read all drug labels carefully.

Using Medicine Safely

While medicines can be helpful, they can also be harmful. Following safety rules when taking medicines can lower your chances of ever being harmed by them.

9:4 Medicine Safety

You should be safe with all kinds of medicines. Remember that all medicines are drugs.

Sometimes, a person does not use medicines in a safe way. A person may take a medicine incorrectly or by mistake. This is called drug misuse. Suppose a person does not read a drug label carefully. This person might take the wrong medicine by mistake. This person is misusing the drug.

What is drug misuse?

Suppose a person is not feeling well. The person takes twice as much medicine as is directed on the label. This person is hoping that twice as much medicine will help him or her feel better faster. This example is also drug misuse. The person is taking the medicine incorrectly. Drug misuse can be harmful to a person's health.

What is drug abuse?

Sometimes, a person uses a drug for reasons other than illness. The person does not need the drug. He or she takes the drug on purpose to help him or her feel good or relax. This is called drug abuse. Drug abuse also can harm a person's health.

There are ways you can prevent drug misuse and drug abuse. Learn to use medicines safely. Follow the safety rules listed in Table 9–1 at the top of page 125.

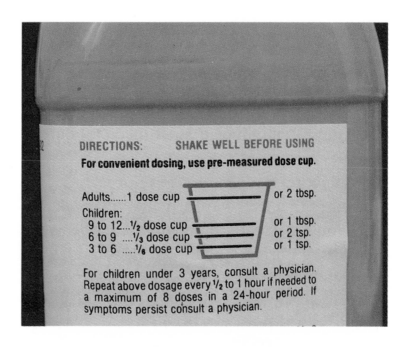

FIGURE 9–6. Use drugs correctly.

Table 9-1

Drug Safety
• Take medicine only when a grown-up gives it to you.
• Take prescription medicine that is ordered just for you.
• Always put medicine back in its own package.
• Read and follow drug labels carefully. Read the directions on the drug package. Keep the label on the package. The label has the directions for safe use. The label tells the last date the medicine should be used. Never use the medicine after this date.
• Always check the package of an over-the-counter drug. Buy only those medicines that have not been opened. Then you know no one has changed the drug.

9:5 Side Effects

All drugs change the way a person's body works. Medicines are taken to change the body in ways that are healthful and desired. However, sometimes a medicine can change the body in ways that are harmful and not desired. The medicine causes a side effect. A **side effect** is a body change that is not wanted. The same medicine may cause side effects in one person but not another. A rash is an example of a side effect.

Suppose you have an illness. The doctor may tell you to take a medicine to help relieve symptoms. The medicine causes you to feel dizzy. Being dizzy is a side effect. Suppose you take a medicine that upsets your stomach. This can also be a side effect.

Maybe you need to take two medicines at the same time. Neither medicine caused a side effect when you took it alone. However, when you took the medicines together you got a stomachache. Taking two medicines together may cause side effects.

What should you do if you have a side effect?

Tell your parents when a medicine gives you a side effect. Your parents can ask your doctor what to do.

Think About It

4. Why should you read the drug label before taking any medicine?
5. Why should you tell your parents if you have a side effect from medicine?

Life Skills

► Do not use another person's prescription drug.
► Carefully read labels on prescription and over-the-counter drugs.
► Use medicines only when given by a grown-up.
► Always put medicine back in its own package.
► Tell your parents if a medicine you are taking produces a side effect.

Health Highlights

Pharmacist

Mark Jones plays an important part in helping people stay healthy. He works in a drugstore as a pharmacist. Each day many people come to Mark to get their prescriptions filled. Mark reads the prescription order. He makes sure the information written by the doctor is complete. Then he makes sure the correct medicine is prepared. The medicine is placed in a container. He places the information about the medicine on a label. The label is placed on the container.

Mark went to college to learn how to be a pharmacist. He studied many science courses. He learned the names of many drugs. He learned how drugs work in the body. You may think about becoming a pharmacist.

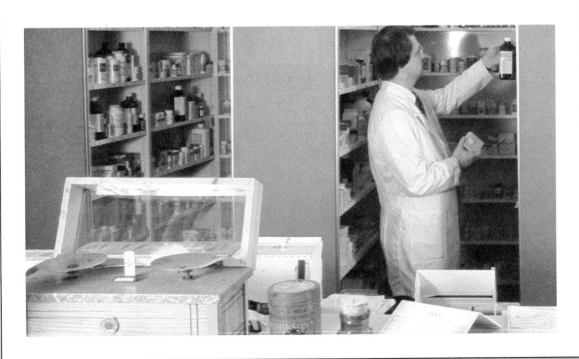

Chapter 9 Review

Summary

1. Drugs can change the way you feel, think, and act. *9:1*
2. Some over-the-counter drugs may help when you are ill. *9:2*
3. Prescription drugs are ordered by a doctor or dentist and prepared for only one person. *9:3*
4. There are rules for the safe use of medicine. *9:4*
5. Parents should be told when you have a side effect from medicine. *9:5*

Words for Health

Complete each sentence with the correct word.
DO NOT WRITE IN THIS BOOK.

cure	prescription
drug	prescription drug
medicine	side effect
over-the-counter (OTC) drugs	symptom
pharmacist	

1. The order a medical doctor or dentist writes for a drug is called a ____.
2. A ____ is an unwanted body change from a medicine.
3. To ____ is to make well.
4. A substance that changes the way the body works is a ____.
5. A ____ is a drug ordered by a doctor or a dentist.
6. Drugs you can buy without a doctor's written order are ____.
7. A drug used to treat an illness or injury is a ____.

8. A signal that you may be sick is a ____.

9. A ____ prepares medicine that a doctor has ordered.

Reviewing Health

1. How can medicines be helpful?

2. Where can OTC drugs be purchased?

3. What is the purpose of a drug label?

4. How do drug misuse and drug abuse differ?

5. What are examples of side effects?

Using Life Skills

Use the life skills from this chapter to respond to the following questions.

Situation: You have been ill. Your parent takes you to the doctor to be checked. The doctor orders a prescription drug to help you feel better. You are given the medicine at home. The medicine causes you to get a rash.

1. Why should you tell your parent about the rash?

2. What might your parent do if you get a rash?

Extending Health

1. Draw a poster that shows how it is wrong to misuse or abuse drugs. Write a saying for your poster.

2. Have your parents show you an over-the-counter and a prescription drug label. Talk about any warnings you find on the labels. Find out what side effects a person might have if they take these medicines.

Kinds of Drugs

There are many different kinds of drugs. Some drugs are illegal because they are harmful. Can you name some harmful drugs? Do you know how they affect the body?

Chapter 10

STUDENT OBJECTIVES: You will be able to

● *discuss how stimulants and depressants harm the body.*

● *describe why drugs like marijuana are dangerous.*

In this chapter, you will study what effects harmful drugs can have on the body. You will study why it is important not to use illegal drugs.

Stimulants and Depressants

Drugs can have many different effects on the body. Drugs can slow down the way the body works. They can speed up the way the body works. These effects can be harmful.

10:1 Caffeine

Think about a time when you have felt excited. You may have felt your heart beating fast. You may have felt nervous. You may have begun to sweat. This is a natural way for your body to react when you are excited.

FIGURE 10–1. Coffee contains a drug called caffeine.

There are certain kinds of drugs that can cause these same feelings in your body. These drugs are called stimulants (STIHM yuh luntz). A **stimulant** is a drug that speeds up the action of body organs. This kind of drug causes the body to work harder than it usually does.

What is caffeine?

Caffeine (ka FEEN) is a stimulant drug found in chocolate, coffee and some tea, and soft drinks. Many doctors believe that too much caffeine can be harmful to your health. Caffeine can keep you awake at night and make you feel nervous. It may also cause headaches and stomachaches. Doctors are studying whether or not caffeine is related to certain diseases.

Try to limit the amount of caffeine you eat or drink. Limit the amount of chocolate candy you eat. Drink fruit juices or soft drinks that do not have caffeine.

ACTIVITY

Finding Caffeine

Cut out pictures of all kinds of foods and drinks. Separate the pictures into two groups. One group will contain caffeine. The other group will not contain caffeine. Make a large poster with these two groups.

10:2 Cocaine and Crack

Certain drugs harm people. Laws have been passed to make certain drugs illegal to have, use, or buy. Illegal means against the law.

One illegal drug is cocaine (koh KAYN). **Cocaine** is a stimulant drug that comes from the coca plant. Cocaine is very dangerous. It causes heart rate to increase rapidly. The heart can stop beating during or after cocaine use. Using cocaine can cause instant death.

Crack is a form of cocaine. Users of crack may experience the same effects as cocaine users. They may suffer heart damage and death as a result of using crack.

FIGURE 10-2. Crack is a form of cocaine.

FIGURE 10–3. Some people need help to stop using drugs.

People who use cocaine and crack often have health problems. They often appear to have a cold. They may lose weight and not be able to sleep well. People who use cocaine and crack also may feel restless and very sad.

Both cocaine and crack are dangerous in another way. The use of these drugs will cause drug dependence. **Drug dependence** is a need to continue to use a drug. People who have drug dependence usually need help to stop using drugs.

What is drug dependence?

10:3 Depressants

A **depressant** (dih PRES unt) is a drug that slows down the work of body organs. The body does not work as it usually does. Depressants cause the heart to beat slower than usual. They also cause a person to feel tired.

Alcohol is a depressant drug. Many people drink alcohol. Beer and wine are drinks that have alcohol. Alcohol is not digested like other foods. It goes straight into the blood. The blood carries alcohol to the brain.

A person can feel the effects of alcohol right away. Once in the brain, alcohol causes body activities to slow down. Because it is a depressant, it may cause a person to feel sleepy. A person may also feel sad. Some people become loud and talk a lot when they drink alcohol. It is best to say NO to depressant drugs like alcohol.

How might alcohol make a person feel?

1. How can caffeine change the way a person's body works?
2. Why is it dangerous for someone to use cocaine?
3. What is a depressant?

Think About It

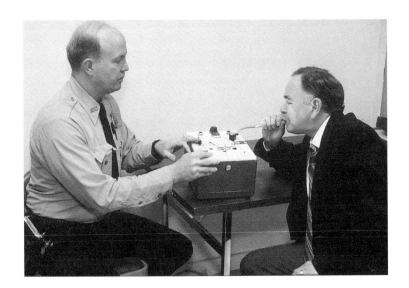

FIGURE 10–4.
Alcohol is a drug that slows body activities.

Avoiding Illegal Drugs

All illegal drugs are dangerous. They should never be used. Say NO to using any illegal drug.

10:4 Marijuana

Marijuana (mer uh WAHN uh) is a harmful drug made from parts of the cannabis (KAN uh bus) plant. It is illegal to buy, sell, or use marijuana.

Marijuana contains hundreds of substances. Many of these substances harm the lungs, the brain, and other parts of the body. Marijuana changes the way a person thinks. People who use this drug may not be able to study. They may not be able to remember what they learn in school.

Marijuana also causes muscles in the body to not work as they should. This can result in accidents.

How does marijuana affect thinking?

FIGURE 10–5. Using marijuana can affect the way a person thinks.

10:5 Saying NO to Illegal Drugs

You can show yourself and others that you care about yourself. You can use refusal skills to say NO to illegal drugs.

- Look directly at the person.
- Say NO clearly and firmly.
  "No, I will not use drugs."
- Give a reason for your decision.
  "Drugs are harmful."
- Show you mean what you say.
  Walk away from anyone who might be trying to get you to use an illegal drug.
- Do not change your mind.

Always tell a parent, teacher, or another grown-up you trust when someone offers you drugs.

FIGURE 10–6. You can learn how to say NO to harmful drugs.

4. Why is marijuana illegal?
5. How can you say NO if someone offers you illegal drugs?

Think About It

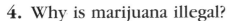 **Life Skills**

- ▶ Limit products that have caffeine.
- ▶ Say NO to using any illegal drug.
- ▶ Tell a grown-up if someone offers you an illegal drug.

Chapter 10 Review

Summary

1. Stimulant drugs speed up the work of body organs. *10:1*
2. Cocaine and crack are illegal drugs that are stimulants. *10:2*
3. Depressant drugs slow down the work of body organs. *10:3*
4. Marijuana is a harmful and illegal drug. *10:4*
5. The responsible choice is to say NO to taking any illegal drug. *10:5*

Words for Health

Complete each sentence with the correct word.
DO NOT WRITE IN THIS BOOK.

caffeine	drug dependence
cocaine	marijuana
crack	stimulant
depressant	

1. ____ is a harmful drug from parts of the cannabis plant.
2. A ____ is a drug that slows down the work of body organs.
3. ____ is a person's need for a drug.
4. ____ is an illegal stimulant that comes from the coca plant.
5. ____ is a stimulant drug found in some kinds of soft drinks.

6. ___ is a drug that is a form of cocaine.
7. A ___ is a drug that speeds up the work of body organs.

1. What products contain caffeine?
2. Why is using crack dangerous?
3. How do depressants make a person feel?
4. How does marijuana affect thinking?
5. What should you do if someone offers you an illegal drug?

Use the life skills from this chapter to respond to the following questions.

Situation: You and your friend are walking home from school. A teenager who lives in your neighborhood calls you and your friend over. This person offers you and your friend a marijuana cigarette.
1. What should you and your friend do?
2. Why is it harmful for someone to use marijuana?

Bring an article from a newspaper to class about an illegal drug. Describe the effects of this drug.

Alcohol and Tobacco

You make choices that affect your health every day. If you care for your health, what choice will you make about the use of alcohol? What choice will you make about the use of tobacco?

Chapter 11

STUDENT OBJECTIVES: *You will be able to*

- *discuss why alcohol is a dangerous drug.*
- *make a choice to avoid using tobacco.*

Recent studies show that more and more people are saying NO to using alcohol and tobacco. They are choosing to have good health.

Alcohol

You want to be your best at all times. One way to do this is to avoid using harmful drugs.

11:1 Alcohol and Your Body

Some drinks contain alcohol. **Alcohol** is a harmful drug. It can harm brain cells. It can destroy the liver. It can cause cancer. People who drink alcohol may have many health problems.

People who drink alcohol may make poor decisions. Alcohol changes the way the brain works. A person who drinks alcohol may not remember things clearly.

People who drink alcohol are more likely to have accidents. This is because alcohol affects how quickly a person can move. Many deaths from car accidents, drowning, and crimes are the result of someone's drinking.

FIGURE 11–1. Many people are trying to prevent car accidents that are caused by people who have been drinking alcohol.

11:2 Saying NO to Alcohol ⎯⎯⎯

Many adults choose not to drink alcohol. They feel this is the best choice. They choose to protect their health.

FIGURE 11–2.
Families can have fun without the use of alcohol.

At your age, drinking alcohol is not a responsible choice. It is illegal. You are too young to buy alcohol. Your body would be affected by alcohol more quickly than an adult's body.

There are many ways to say NO to drinking alcohol. You can tell a person that you do not want to harm your body. You can say that drinking alcohol is illegal. You can say that you want to obey your parents and choose not to drink alcohol.

When you say NO to drinking alcohol, you are showing that you can make a responsible decision. You are showing that you care about yourself and your family.

Why is alcohol not a responsible choice for someone your age?

1. Why is alcohol dangerous?
2. What are three ways to say NO to alcohol?

Think About It

143

Tobacco

More people are making the choice not to smoke. Fewer young people are choosing to start smoking. They know tobacco (tuh BAK oh) is a harmful drug.

11:3 Smoking and Your Body

People who smoke cigarettes, pipes, and cigars use tobacco. **Tobacco** is a plant that contains the harmful drug nicotine (NIHK uh teen). **Nicotine** is a stimulant drug found in tobacco. Nicotine from tobacco enters the body when a person inhales smoke. Nicotine in the smoke enters the lungs. It passes into the blood and then to other parts of the body.

What is nicotine?

FIGURE 11-3.
Smoke contains nicotine, which is harmful to health.

FIGURE 11–4. There are warning labels on cigarette packages.

Nicotine makes the heart beat faster than it should. If a person's heart beats faster than it should, the heart will have to work too hard. Nicotine and other drugs in tobacco cause the blood vessels to become narrow. The heart must work harder to pump blood through the blood vessels. Blood does not flow as easily to all parts of the body. Body cells receive less oxygen.

Tobacco smoke also contains tar. **Tar** is a brown, sticky substance in tobacco that is harmful. Tar in the lungs can result in lung cancer.

What is tar?

Tobacco smoke also can be harmful to people who do not smoke. Suppose you are in a room with people who smoke. The smoke in the air you inhale affects you. Your heart may beat faster. Your eyes may water and your throat may become sore.

Many people who smoke would like to stop. This is not an easy thing to do. Most smokers become dependent on nicotine. They may need help to learn how to stop smoking. There are places in your community that offer programs to help people stop smoking. Your school nurse knows the names of many places that offer help.

ACTIVITY

A No-Smoking Ad

Look through a magazine. Think about how you can use pictures to show how smoking is harmful. Cut and paste pictures on a piece of paper to make a No-Smoking ad. Display your ad in the classroom.

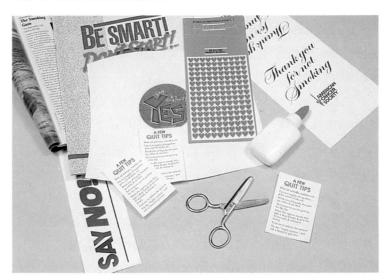

FIGURE 11–5. Many people choose not to smoke.

11:4 Saying NO to Smoking ___

Many people choose not to smoke. They do not want their friends to smoke. They know that smoking is harmful.

Why do many people choose not to smoke?

Many people do not want to be in places where others smoke. They may ask others not to smoke in their homes. Smoking is not allowed in many public areas. In many work places, rules have been made that do not allow smoking. Also, in some areas, laws have been passed that do not allow smoking in schools or on school grounds. These rules and laws have been made to protect people's health. People realize that smoking can be harmful to others.

If someone asks you to smoke, say NO. No one can force you to smoke. A good friend would not want you to harm your health. Choosing friends who do not smoke will help you avoid smoking.

11:5 Smokeless Tobacco

Not all tobacco is smoked. Some tobacco can be chewed. **Smokeless tobacco** is tobacco that is placed in the mouth rather than smoked. This tobacco is used by putting a small amount between the gums and cheek.

Some people think smokeless tobacco is safe. They think it is safe because smoke is not inhaled. However, it affects the body in many of the same ways as tobacco that is smoked. Nicotine and other drugs in smokeless tobacco cause the heart to work harder. People who use smokeless tobacco also become dependent on nicotine. Smokeless tobacco can cause cancer of the mouth and throat.

Smokeless tobacco contains sugar. The sugar can cause tooth decay and harm the gums. Smokeless tobacco stains the teeth. It causes bad breath. It is not safe to use.

What does smokeless tobacco do to a person's teeth?

FIGURE 11–6.
Smokeless tobacco is harmful to health.

FIGURE 11–7. Using tobacco can cause cancer.

If someone offers you smokeless tobacco, say NO. Tell the person the harmful effects of using tobacco products. Feel good about yourself. Show yourself and others that you can make responsible decisions.

Think About It

3. How does nicotine in tobacco smoke reach parts of the body?
4. Why is it healthful to choose friends who do not smoke?
5. How does smokeless tobacco harm the body?

Life Skills

▶ Do not drink alcohol.
▶ Do not use tobacco products.
▶ Use refusal skills to say NO to drinking alcohol and using tobacco.

Chapter 11 Review

Summary

1. Alcohol is a harmful drug to use. *11:1*
2. There are many ways to say NO to drinking alcohol. *11:2*
3. Smoking harms many parts of the body. *11:3*
4. There are ways to say NO to smoking. *11:4*
5. Smokeless tobacco can harm the heart, mouth, teeth, and gums. *11:5*

Words for Health

Complete each sentence with the correct word.
DO NOT WRITE IN THIS BOOK.

alcohol
nicotine
smokeless tobacco
tar
tobacco

1. A plant that contains the harmful drug nicotine is ___.
2. A harmful drug that can destroy a person's liver is ___.
3. ___ is placed in the mouth.
4. A brown, sticky substance in tobacco that harms the lungs is ___.
5. A harmful stimulant drug found in tobacco is ___.

1. What are two effects of alcohol on the body?
2. Why is drinking alcohol not a responsible choice for someone your age?
3. How does nicotine affect the heart?
4. Why do many people choose not to smoke?
5. What should a person do if someone offers him or her smokeless tobacco?

Use the life skills from this chapter to respond to the following questions.

Situation: You walk into a family restaurant with your parents. Your parents are asked where they would like to sit. In one section is a sign that says No Smoking. In another section, a sign says Smoking Section.

1. Why might the responsible choice be to sit in the No-Smoking section?
2. Why might you and your parents feel good in making the choice to sit in the No-Smoking section?

Interview your parents. Find out how they made choices about smoking. List their reasons.

Diseases and Disorders

Did you know . . .

▶ germs can cause disease?

▶ your body has defenses against harmful germs?

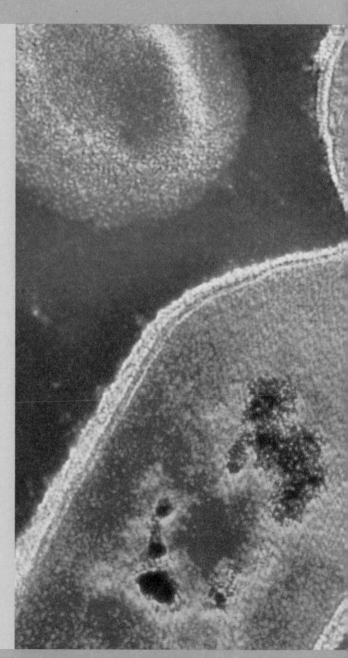

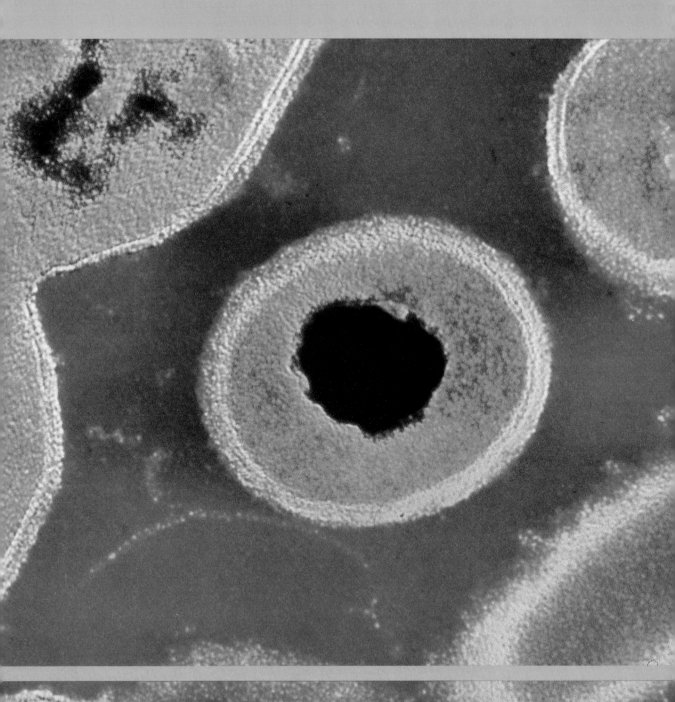

Unit 7

Disease and Your Body

Germs that enter your body can harm your health. Germs can cause disease. Your body works to protect itself from disease. You can take action to protect your body from disease.

Chapter 12

STUDENT OBJECTIVES: *You will be able to*
- *discuss how germs enter the body.*
- *describe how the body protects itself from germs.*

What does it feel like to be healthy? You may play with friends. You may feel happy and enjoy life. There are ways to stay healthy. You can follow certain rules that help keep you healthy.

How Germs Enter Your Body

Germs may harm your health. These germs can be spread in many ways. Sometimes germs get into your body.

12:1 Germs and Your Body

Germs are very tiny living things. They are so small that you need a microscope to see them. They are found everywhere. Some germs cause disease.

FIGURE 12–1. Rest helps your body become stronger when you are sick.

What is disease?

If germs get inside you, your body provides warmth, food, and water. As a result, germs can live and grow in your body.

Your body kills most of the harmful germs that grow inside it. Sometimes it cannot kill enough of these germs. When too many germs begin to grow inside your body, they cause disease. **Disease** is a condition of your body that keeps it from working as it should.

Your body may need help to fight germs. Medicine made from certain drugs can kill some of these germs. Your doctor may give you medicine when you are sick. A strong body can fight more germs. Rest helps your body become stronger.

12:2 How Germs Spread

Germs can be spread by people. When a person sneezes or coughs, germs enter the air. You may breathe in these germs. The germs then grow in number in your body. You may become sick. Colds, flu, and chicken pox are some diseases that can be spread by people.

Germs can live on some objects. Suppose your sister has flu. When she drinks from a glass, some of her germs stay on the glass. Later, if you use your sister's glass, some of her germs may enter your body. These germs may cause you to become ill.

Germs can be spread in other ways. Animals can spread germs. Suppose an animal bites you. Your skin is broken by the bite. Germs from the animal can enter your body through the broken skin. You may become sick.

Where can germs live?

FIGURE 12–2. You can help prevent the spread of germs.

157

FIGURE 12–3.
Flies can leave germs on food.

Insects can spread germs. A fly has germs on its body. If it lands on food, some germs are left on the food. Suppose you eat the food. Germs that are on the food enter your body. You may become ill.

Some germs live in water. Suppose you swim in a lake. You may swallow some of the lake water. If the water has germs, you may become sick. The water in which people swim should be tested to make sure it is safe.

How could you get germs from lake water?

Water that comes into your home and school should be safe to drink. It is cleaned and tested before it is piped into houses or other buildings.

Think About It

1. How does your body help prevent disease?
2. How can a fly spread disease?

Protection Against Disease

There are different ways you can be protected from disease. When you were very young, you were given shots to protect you from certain diseases. You probably will not get those diseases. Your body can also protect itself against some diseases.

12:3 Viruses and Bacteria _____

Different germs cause different kinds of diseases. Viruses (VI rus uz) and bacteria (bak TIHR ee uh) are different kinds of germs. A **virus** is the smallest kind of germ. A virus cannot be killed by taking medicine. **Bacteria** are one-celled germs. Bacteria can be killed by taking certain kinds of medicine.

What is a virus?

Think about the last time you had a cold. Maybe you sneezed and had a runny nose. A cold is a disease caused by a virus. Maybe you had a sore throat. A sore throat may be caused by a virus or a type of bacteria.

a
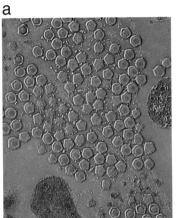

b
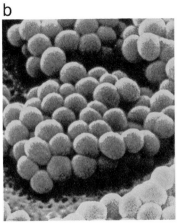

FIGURE 12-4.
(a) Viruses and (b) bacteria are different kinds of germs.

FIGURE 12–5. A person with flu may have a fever.

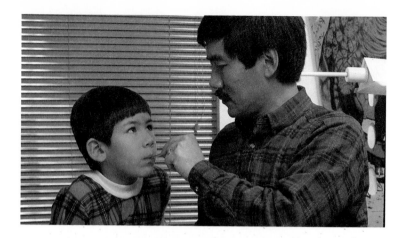

Flu is another disease caused by a virus. People with flu may have a cough, an upset stomach, body aches, fever, and chills.

What is chicken pox?

Many people your age may have had chicken pox. Chicken pox is a disease caused by a virus. Red, watery spots that itch appear on the skin. If you should get chicken pox, you should not scratch the spots. There are medicines to use for chicken pox to stop the itch. Never take aspirin when you have chicken pox or flu. The aspirin may cause you to get a more serious disease.

12:4 Body Defenses

Suppose you are at a football game. You hear people yell "defense." They want their team to defend their goal. To defend means to protect or guard. Each team tries to protect its goal. Your body has ways to protect itself from germs. Your body has defenses.

Body defenses are body actions or parts that protect you from disease. Your skin is one kind of defense. It can stop germs from entering your body. If your skin is not cut or broken, germs cannot enter your body through your skin.

Blood cells are another defense against disease. If some germs do enter your body, certain cells in your blood can kill the germs.

Another body defense is an antibody (ANT ih bahd ee). An **antibody** is a substance in your blood that kills germs. Your body makes a different antibody to kill each kind of germ.

What is an antibody?

Antibodies are made by your body in two ways. Each time you have an illness caused by a germ, your blood makes antibodies to kill that kind of germ. Antibodies are also made after you are given a vaccine (vak SEEN).

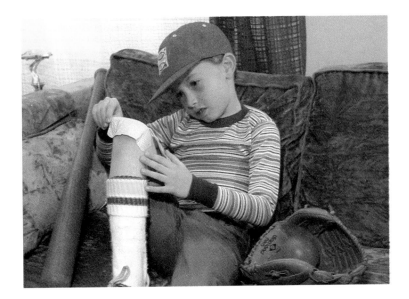

FIGURE 12–6. Germs can enter your body through a cut.

FIGURE 12–7. A vaccine can help protect you from getting a certain disease.

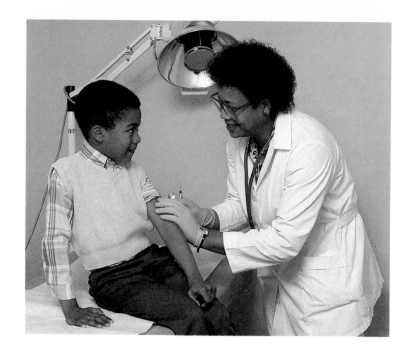

What is a vaccine?

A **vaccine** is a substance made with dead or weak germs. There are different kinds of vaccines. Each vaccine can protect you from a certain kind of disease.

When you were very young, you were given different vaccines. These vaccines protect your body from getting some kinds of disease. Suppose germs that cause measles enter your body. If you have had a measles vaccine, your blood will have antibodies against measles. These antibodies kill any measles germs that enter your body.

You also can help protect your body from germs that can cause disease. Wash your hands with soap and water after you use the bathroom and before you eat. Do not get too close to people who are sick. Have regular checkups from your family doctor.

ACTIVITY

Washing Germs Away

Do this experiment in class. Cover your hands with petroleum jelly and then dip them into sand. Gently shake off the extra sand. Pretend that the grains of sand are germs. Wash your hands without using soap. What happened to the sand? Now wash your hands using soap. What happened to the sand? Tell why is it important to always wash with soap.

12:5 Diseases That Are Not Spread

Not all diseases are caused by germs. Cancer and heart disease cannot be spread to others. **Cancer** is a disease in which harmful cells in the body grow in number and attack healthy cells. The harmful cancer cells can destroy parts of the body.

a
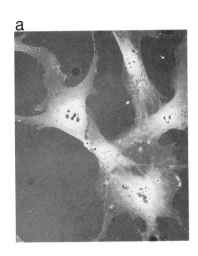

b
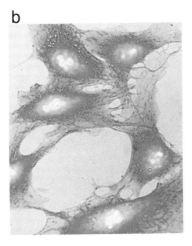

FIGURE 12–8. Notice how (a) cancer cells destroy (b) healthy cells.

FIGURE 12–9. Eat healthful foods to help keep your heart strong.

What is heart disease?

Heart disease is an illness that affects the heart. You can lower your chances of ever getting cancer or heart disease. Keep your body healthy. Do not eat too many fatty and greasy foods. Exercise to keep your heart and body strong.

Think About It

3. Why should you never take aspirin for flu?
4. How does your skin help protect you?
5. How does cancer affect your body?

Life Skills

▶ Wash your hands before eating and after using the bathroom.
▶ Always use soap when washing your hands.
▶ Eat healthful foods and get regular exercise to help prevent cancer and heart disease.

Health Highlights

Dr. Jonas Salk

Dr. Jonas Salk is responsible for saving thousands of lives. Until 1954, a disease called polio caused many deaths. Polio is caused by a virus. When it gets in the body, it causes a person's body to become paralyzed. When a body part is paralyzed, it is numb. There is no feeling in that body part. That body part cannot be used.

Dr. Salk found a way to prevent polio. He spent many hours in a lab doing experiments. He found a way to develop a vaccine for polio. A polio vaccine prevents the polio virus from affecting the body. When you were a baby, you probably received the polio vaccine. When babies receive this vaccine, they are protected against polio.

Chapter 12 Review

Summary

1. Germs can cause disease. *12:1*
2. Germs can be spread by people, animals, insects, and through water. *12:2*
3. Some diseases caused by viruses are the cold, flu, and chicken pox. *12:3*
4. Different body defenses can protect you from disease. *12:4*
5. Cancer and heart disease are diseases that cannot be spread to others. *12:5*

Words for Health

Complete each sentence with the correct word below. DO NOT WRITE IN THIS BOOK.

antibody
bacteria
cancer
disease
germs
heart disease
vaccine
virus

1. ____ is a disease in which harmful cells attack healthy cells.
2. A ____ is a condition of the body that keeps it from working well.
3. The smallest kind of germ is called a ____.
4. One-celled germs that can be killed by taking certain kinds of medicine are called ____.

5. Dead or weak germs are found in a ___.
6. An ___ found in blood kills germs.
7. ___ are tiny living things.
8. ___ is an illness that affects the heart.

Reviewing Health

1. What conditions are needed for germs to grow?
2. What are two ways diseases are spread?
3. How do viruses and bacteria differ?
4. What are two kinds of body defenses?
5. How can you lower your chances of ever having heart disease?

Using Life Skills

Use the life skills from this chapter to respond to the following questions.

Situation: You are at a family picnic. Some of the food is uncovered. You notice that flies land on some of the food and then fly away.

1. Why is it unsafe to leave food uncovered?
2. What should you do to help keep food safe to eat if you are at a picnic?

Extending Health

1. Find a book in your school library about a person who discovered a cure for a disease. Read this book and write a report about this person.
2. Write a report about a certain kind of disease. Your report may include the cause, signs, prevention, and treatment of that disease.

Consumer and Personal Health

Did you know . . .

▶ ads try to convince you to buy health products?

▶ regular medical and dental checkups help keep you healthy?

168

Personal Health Choices

Have you had a health checkup lately? Have you ever been in a hospital? If so, you have used health services. A consumer uses health products and services to help keep healthy.

Chapter 13

STUDENT OBJECTIVES: *You will be able to*

- *discuss who a consumer is and what products are used for grooming.*
- *make and follow a plan to keep skin, hair, and nails healthy.*

Many products can be used to help keep you healthy. Choosing the best products for you and using them regularly are important. Your physical, mental, and social health can be improved by proper care of your body.

You as a Consumer

The magazines you read and the TV programs you watch have ads for products to keep you neat and clean. Other ads offer products that may affect the way you feel. How will those ads affect the choices you make? What questions should you ask to make the best choices?

13:1   Who Is a Consumer?

A **consumer** is a person who buys and uses products and services. To be a wise consumer, you need to be careful about your personal health choices.

As a wise consumer, you would look carefully at a product you are thinking about buying. You would want to know how much the product costs. You would decide if you really need the product. You might look at other similar products. Then you could decide which product is a wise choice.

13:2   Health Products

Using health products is an important part of being healthy. Some health products help you be well-groomed. A person who is well-groomed has a neat and clean appearance. Being neat and clean helps you feel good about yourself. Being clean can help prevent illness. Being well-groomed also may help your relationships with others.

FIGURE 13–1. A consumer buys and uses products.

Listed below are examples of some health products you and your parents might buy.

Health Products		
toothbrush	cotton swabs	hairbrush
toothpaste	fingernail brush	comb
dental floss	fingernail file	tissues
soap	toenail clipper	shampoo

Which products would you use for hair care? Which products would you use for dental health care? What would you use to clean and care for your fingernails?

ACTIVITY

Ads You Like

Cut out five ads for health products. Paste each ad on a sheet of colored paper. Tell what you like about each ad. Does the ad make you want to buy this product? Why would you use this product? Would using the product help you stay healthy?

Think About It

1. When are you a consumer?
2. What questions should you ask about a health product you are thinking about buying?

Caring for Your Body

Caring for your skin, hair, and nails is important for your appearance and health. Good posture and sleeping habits also are needed for good health.

13:3 Your Skin

Skin is the organ that covers your body. Your skin helps you stay healthy. Special nerve cells in your skin help you feel how hot or cold an object is when you touch it.

Your skin also helps control your body temperature. When you are warm, blood vessels in your skin get larger. This causes more blood to come to the surface of the skin. Heat escapes from your blood as it flows near the skin's surface. This helps keep you cool. When you are cold, blood vessels in your skin get smaller. Less blood comes to the skin's surface. Less heat is lost from the surface of the skin. This helps keep you warm.

Your skin has two layers. The **epidermis** (ep uh DUR mus) is the outer layer of skin. You can see your epidermis. Some cells in the epidermis are dead. Dead cells are always falling off or being rubbed off. Cells under the dead cells are living cells. Living skin cells keep taking the place of dead skin cells.

How does your skin help you stay healthy?

FIGURE 13–2. Your skin is made of cells.

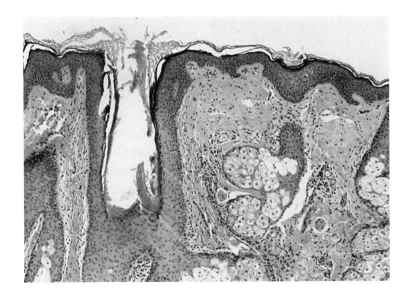

FIGURE 13–3. The dermis is the layer of skin under the epidermis.

The **dermis** (DUR mus) is the inner layer of skin. Most of the time, you do not see the dermis. Blood vessels are in the dermis. Blood carries food and oxygen to the cells of the skin.

There are many ways to keep your skin healthy. You can eat green, leafy vegetables and foods from the meat group. These foods are needed for healthy skin. Substances in these foods are used to make new skin cells and to keep your skin smooth.

What can you eat to keep skin healthy?

Your skin needs to be kept clean. You should wash your skin using soap and water. Soap breaks down the oils on the skin. Dirt and germs might be trapped in these oils. Soap and water help remove perspiration (pur spuh RAY shun). **Perspiration** is the salty liquid waste that comes out of your skin. If perspiration is not removed, dirt and germs can collect on the skin.

175

13:4 Your Hair

Hair covers much of your body. Most of it grows on your head. Your hair grows from tubes in the skin called hair follicles (FAHL ih kulz). Oil glands are near the hair follicles. An **oil gland** is a gland that makes body oil. This oil keeps your hair from becoming dry. The oil also helps keep your skin soft. Hair acts to hold in body heat. It also protects your skin from the sun.

What is an oil gland?

There are ways to keep your hair healthy. Comb and brush your hair daily to keep it neat, clean, and healthy.

Wash your hair at least twice a week to remove dirt and oil. If your hair is oily, you may need to wash it more often.

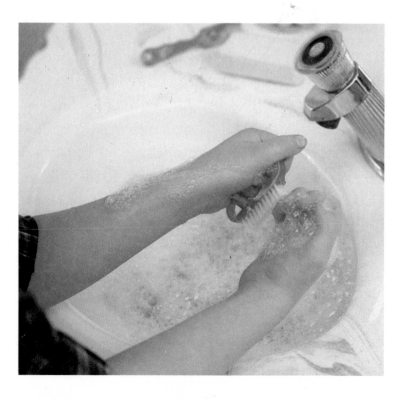

FIGURE 13–4.
Washing your hands helps remove germs.

Rub shampoo into your hair and scalp with your fingertips. Your **scalp** is the skin that covers the top of your head. Rinse your hair. Shampoo and rinse again. Make sure you rinse out all the shampoo. Shampoo left in the hair may make your scalp itch.

FIGURE 13–5.
Washing your hair removes dirt and oil.

13:5 Your Nails

Fingernails and toenails are formed by the epidermis. Fingernails are hard tissues that protect the ends of your fingers. Toenails are hard tissues that protect the ends of your toes. Both fingernails and toenails are made mostly of dead cells. You can trim fingernails and toenails without feeling pain.

What are fingernails?

To keep fingernails and toenails healthy, wash them each day. If needed, use a nailbrush to clean under the nails to remove dirt and germs. Keep your nails trimmed.

Do not bite your nails. If there are germs under the nails, they could get into your mouth. You could break the skin around the nails. Your fingers could become sore.

13:6 Your Posture

What is posture?

Posture is the way you sit, stand, and move. Good posture is important for health. When you have good posture, your body organs have more room inside your body. You can breathe easier. Blood flows through your body more easily.

You can have good posture. When you sit, keep your feet flat on the floor. Hold your head up and your shoulders back.

FIGURE 13–6. Work on having good posture.

When you stand and walk, keep your back straight. Hold your head up and your shoulders back. Good posture helps you look and feel your best.

13:7 Sleep and Rest

You need about ten hours of sleep each night. While you sleep, your heart beats slower. You take fewer breaths per minute. Your body makes new cells. When you wake up, you feel rested and look fresh. You have energy for work and play.

Think About It

3. Why should you wash with soap and water?
4. How can you keep your hair healthy?
5. Why should you not bite your fingernails?
6. Why is it important to have good posture?
7. Why do you need sleep and rest?

Life Skills

▶ Read ads for health products carefully.
▶ Take the time and effort to be well-groomed.
▶ Use soap and water to wash your skin.
▶ Wash your hair at least twice a week.
▶ Keep fingernails and toenails clean and trimmed.
▶ Sit, stand, and walk with correct posture.
▶ Get the right amount of rest and sleep.

Chapter 13 Review

Summary

1. A wise consumer is careful about health product choices. *13:1*
2. Choosing and using health products are important parts of being healthy. *13:2*
3. Skin allows you to feel how hot or cold objects are and also helps control your body temperature. *13:3*
4. Hair holds in body heat and protects the skin from the sun. *13:4*
5. Nails protect the ends of your fingers and toes. *13:5*
6. Good posture helps you look and feel your best. *13:6*
7. Sleep and rest allow your body to prepare for more activity. *13:7*

Words for Health

Complete each sentence with the correct word.
DO NOT WRITE IN THIS BOOK.

consumer	perspiration
dermis	posture
epidermis	scalp
oil gland	skin

1. ___ is the salty liquid waste that comes out of your skin.
2. ___ is the way you sit, stand, and move.
3. A ___ is a person who buys and uses products and services.
4. ___ is the organ that covers your body.

5. An ___ is a gland that makes body oil.
6. Your ___ is the skin that covers the top of your head.
7. The ___ is the inner layer of skin.
8. The ___ is the outer layer of skin.

1. Who is a consumer?
2. What are five health products?
3. What are three ways your skin helps you?
4. Why should you rinse your hair thoroughly after shampooing?
5. How should you care for fingernails and toenails?
6. How does correct posture help your body organs?
7. In what three ways does your body change while you sleep?

Use the life skills from this chapter to respond to the following questions.

Situation: You are at the store with your parents. You want to buy a new hairbrush. You look at two hairbrushes that are alike. One is in a very attractive box and costs more than the other one.

1. Which hairbrush would you choose to buy?
2. Why was the one hairbrush in a very attractive box?

Cut out three magazine ads for shampoos. Show the ads to three friends or family members. Ask these people which ad they like best and why. What did you learn?

Having Checkups

It is important to have regular medical and dental checkups. Checkups can help you stay healthy. What do you do daily to keep your body healthy?

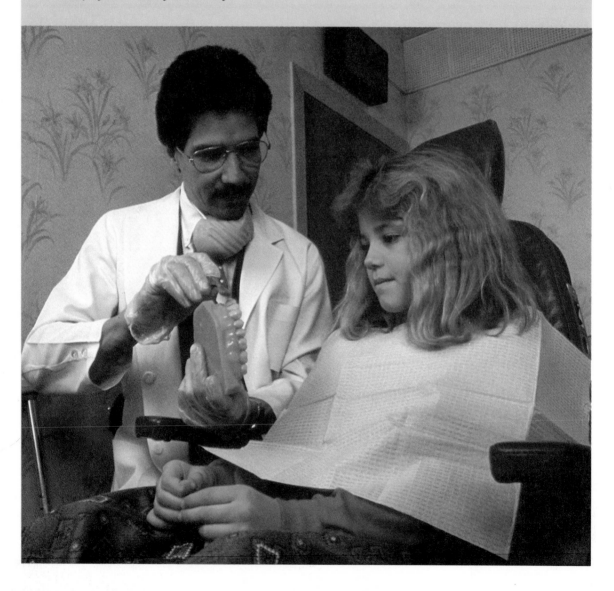

Chapter 14

STUDENT OBJECTIVES: You will be able to
- describe what is included in a medical checkup.
- describe a dental checkup and how to care for teeth.

There are many kinds of health helpers. Two kinds of health helpers are doctors and dentists. You visit your doctor and dentist for regular checkups. These checkups help you keep your body and teeth healthy.

You and Your Doctor

You, your parents, and your doctor are a team. As a team, you work together so that you will have good health. To do this, each of the team members needs information about your health.

14:1 Your Medical Checkup

A **medical checkup** is an examination of your body in which the doctor gains information about your health. Your doctor uses this information to help you and your parents make a plan for good health.

What is a medical checkup?

Which body parts are
checked during a
medical checkup?

During a checkup, the nurse checks and records your height and weight. The doctor checks your eyes and ears. Your nose, mouth, and throat are checked. The doctor listens to the sounds of your heart and lungs. Your doctor will ask questions to learn about your health. You have a checkup to keep your body healthy.

14:2   When You Are Ill

Sometimes you are ill when you go to the doctor. During this kind of visit, the doctor examines you to learn what is making you ill. The doctor will decide on a treatment to help you feel better. A **treatment** is a plan to follow to improve your health. Your parents will help you do what the doctor says.

Think About It

1. Why is it important to have medical checkups?
2. Why do you go to the doctor when you are ill?

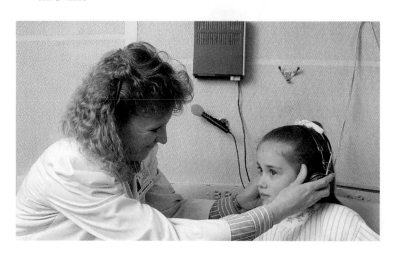

FIGURE 14–1. Have a checkup to keep your body healthy.

FIGURE 14–2. Your teeth are important.

You and Your Dentist

You, your parents, and your dentist are a team. You work together to keep your teeth healthy.

14:3 Your Teeth Are Important

Your teeth help you in many ways. Your teeth and the bones of your face help shape your face. Your teeth help you speak clearly. They also help you break up the food you eat into small pieces.

Your first teeth appear when you are a baby. Your first set of teeth are **primary teeth.** There are twenty primary teeth. They begin to fall out at about age six. After a primary tooth falls out, a larger tooth appears. The larger teeth are called permanent teeth. **Permanent teeth** are your second set of teeth. There are 32 permanent teeth. With proper care, these teeth will last a lifetime.

What are primary teeth?

A tooth has several parts. The **crown** is the part of a tooth you can see. The crown is covered with enamel (ihn AM ul). **Enamel** is a hard, white covering that helps protect the crown. The **pulp** is the center of a tooth. It contains nerves and blood vessels.

The **gum** is the pink tissue around a tooth. The **root** is the part of the tooth under the gum. The root holds the tooth in the jawbone.

ACTIVITY

Parts of the Tooth

Draw a tooth. Use the words above and name the part of the tooth that you can see. Also name the part of the tooth that holds it in the jawbone. Include the name of the center of the tooth.

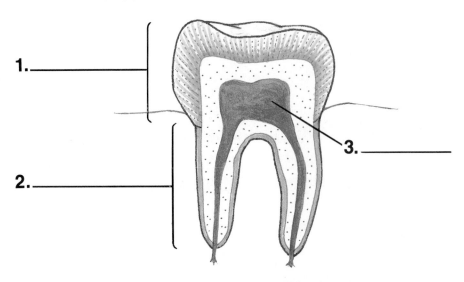

1.

2.

3.

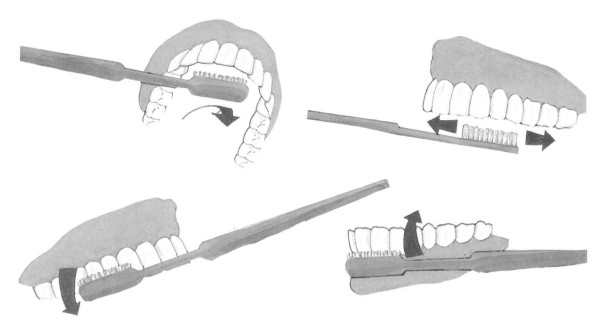

14:4 Brushing and Using Floss

Whenever you eat, small pieces of food get caught between your teeth. These small pieces of food along with germs may form plaque (PLAK). **Plaque** is a sticky material that forms on teeth.

Brushing your teeth helps remove these pieces of food and plaque. You should brush your teeth at least twice a day. If you can, you should brush after every meal. Always try to brush right after you eat something sweet. This helps prevent cavities (KAV ut eez). A **cavity** is a hole in a tooth caused by the germs in plaque.

You need to learn the best way to brush your teeth. After brushing your teeth, remember to gently brush your gums and tongue.

FIGURE 14–3.
Brushing your teeth helps keep them healthy.

Why is it important to brush your teeth?

You need to use dental floss at least once a day. **Dental floss** is a special thin thread used to clean between teeth.

To use floss on your teeth, wrap the floss around the middle finger of each hand. Guide it between your teeth down to the gums. Use it to scrape the sides of your teeth, but do not scrape your gums.

Using dental floss removes any food and plaque that may be left between teeth after you have brushed them. Using dental floss also removes plaque that forms near or under your gums.

Why should you use dental floss?

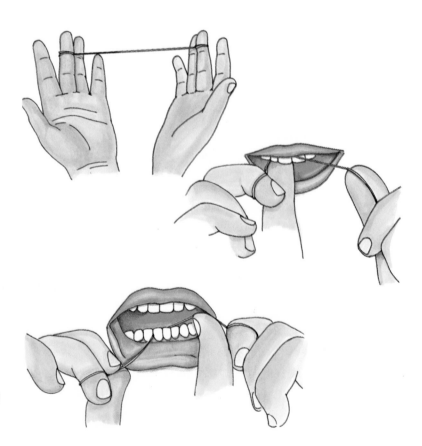

FIGURE 14–4. You should use dental floss at least once a day.

188

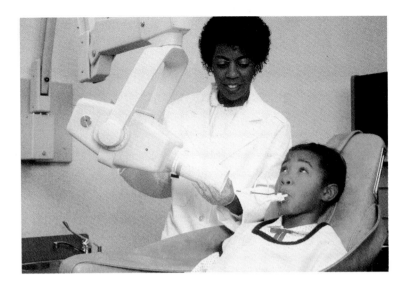

FIGURE 14–5. During a dental checkup, the dentist may take X rays.

14:5 Your Dental Health Plan

Besides brushing and using dental floss, you need to have dental checkups. Every six months you should go to the dentist to have your teeth cleaned and checked. The dentist or dental hygienist (hi JEN ust) will clean your teeth. A dental hygienist is a person who aids a dentist in caring for teeth.

After your teeth are cleaned, the dentist will check for cavities. The dentist may take X rays. A **tooth X ray** is a picture of the inside of a tooth. If you have a cavity, it will show in an X ray. The dentist will fill the cavity. A **filling** is material that fills the hole in a tooth. A filling repairs cavities.

Your dentist may put fluoride (FLOOR ide) on your teeth. **Fluoride** is a substance that helps make teeth strong and less likely to have cavities. Fluoride is found in most drinking water and toothpastes.

How often should you have dental checkups?

How does fluoride help teeth?

Your dentist might talk to you about your diet. Foods from the milk group help make teeth strong. Fruits with vitamin C help keep gums healthy. Your dentist might tell you to limit foods and drinks with sugar and to avoid chewing gum that has sugar.

To protect your teeth, you should wear a mouthguard for sports. A **mouthguard** is a device that covers the teeth to help protect them from injury.

Think About It

3. How do your teeth help you?
4. When should you brush your teeth?
5. Why should you use dental floss daily?
6. Where might you find fluoride for your teeth?

Life Skills

▶ Have regular medical checkups.
▶ Brush your teeth at least twice a day.
▶ Use dental floss at least once a day.
▶ Have a dental checkup every six months.
▶ Choose foods from the milk group and fruits with vitamin C for healthy teeth and gums.
▶ Use toothpastes with fluoride.
▶ Wear a mouthguard when playing sports to protect your teeth.

Pediatrician

Many young people go to a pediatrician (peed ee uh TRISH un) for medical care. A pediatrician is a medical doctor who treats children. Dr. Chen is a pediatrician. She works at a children's hospital taking care of young children. Dr. Chen gives these children checkups to learn about changes in their health. She asks the children questions to learn how they are feeling. This helps her know what to do. Dr. Chen may outline a treatment for a child she examines. She helps the parents understand the treatment. The treatment must be followed exactly.

Dr. Chen enjoys helping children stay healthy. To become a pediatrician, Dr. Chen studied science and health courses. She took a test to get into medical school. First, she became a doctor. Then she studied more to become a pediatrician. Dr. Chen loves her work.

Have you ever thought about being a doctor? If you become a pediatrician, you will work with children and their families. A pediatrician is an important health helper.

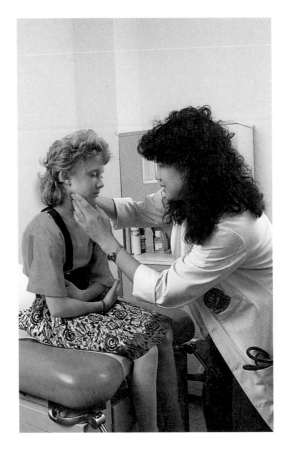

Chapter 14 Review

Summary

1. Your doctor gives you medical checkups to gain information about your health. *14:1*
2. When you are ill, your doctor suggests a treatment to help you get well. *14:2*
3. Your teeth shape your face, help you speak, and help you break foods into smaller pieces. *14:3*
4. Brushing and flossing removes plaque and bits of food from the teeth. *14:4*
5. During a dental checkup, your dentist or hygienist cleans your teeth, takes X rays, and fills any cavities. *14:5*

Words for Health

Complete each sentence with the correct word.
DO NOT WRITE IN THIS BOOK.

cavity	mouthguard
dental floss	permanent teeth
filling	plaque
fluoride	primary teeth
gum	tooth X ray
medical checkup	treatment

1. ___ is sticky material that forms on teeth.
2. A ___ is a plan to follow to improve your health.
3. Your first set of teeth are ___.
4. A ___ is a hole in a tooth caused by the germs in plaque.
5. A ___ is a material that fills the hole in a tooth.

6. A ___ is an examination of your body in which the doctor gains information about your health.
7. ___ is a substance that helps make teeth strong and less likely to have cavities.
8. ___ is a special thin thread used to clean between teeth.
9. A ___ is a picture of the inside of a tooth.
10. A ___ is a device that protects your teeth.
11. ___ are your second set of teeth.
12. ___ is the pink tissue around a tooth.

Reviewing Health

1. What might happen during a medical checkup?
2. How can a doctor help when you are ill?
3. Which set of teeth should last a lifetime?
4. Why should you floss your teeth?
5. Why does a dentist take X rays?

Using Life Skills

Use the life skills from this chapter to respond to the following questions.

Situation: You visit your dentist for a checkup. You have too much plaque on your teeth. The dentist looks at your tooth X rays and finds a cavity.
1. What will the dentist do to take better care of your teeth?
2. What might you do to take better care of your teeth?

Extending Health

Write a report about a dental hygienist.

Safety and First Aid

Did you know . . .

▶ following safety rules can help keep you healthy?

▶ you can help yourself and others if you know first aid?

Accident Prevention

There has been an accident. Someone was careless, and people were injured. It is always important to follow safety rules to help avoid accidents.

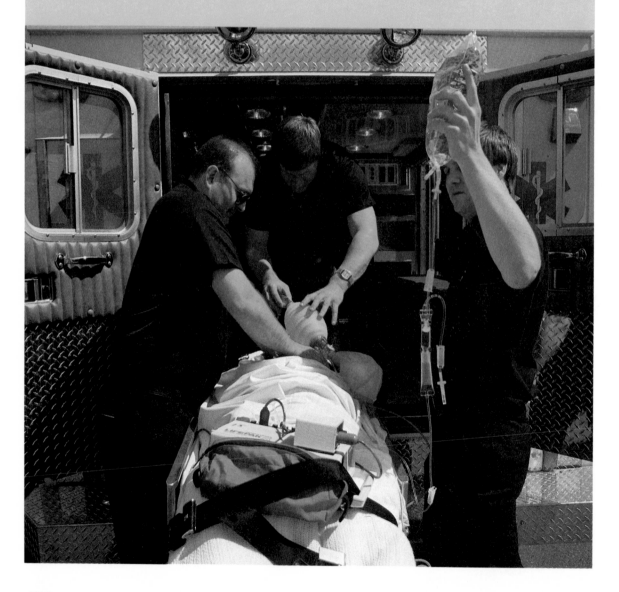

Chapter 15

STUDENT OBJECTIVES: *You will be able to*

- *describe how to be safe when you are a passenger in a car or bus or when riding your bike.*
- *discuss ways to stay safe in your community.*

Accidents happen when people least expect them. It is important to follow safety rules to help avoid accidents. By following safety rules, it may be possible to avoid serious injury.

Safety on the Road

Whether you are a passenger in a car or riding your bike, safety is always important. You can take steps to protect yourself and others.

15:1 Safety in a Car or Bus

An **accident** is something unexpected that happens and may cause injury. Accidents often happen because someone is careless. A car accident can happen when someone does not follow a safe driving rule.

What is an accident?

197

FIGURE 15–1. A safety belt keeps you from being thrown from your seat.

What is a safety belt?

During a sudden stop or accident, you are in danger of being injured. You can help prevent injury caused by a car accident. One way is to always wear a safety belt. A **safety belt** is a strap in a car that keeps you from being thrown from your seat. A safety belt may have a lap belt and a shoulder belt. Most states require people to wear safety belts. It is a law that helps keep people safe.

There are other ways to keep safe while riding in a car. Always lock the car door. Do not stick any part of your body outside the window. Do not disturb the person who is driving.

There are also ways to practice safety when you ride on a bus. Always sit back in your seat. Do not stand up when the bus is moving. Keep hands and objects away from windows. Do not play around with others. Do not disturb the bus driver.

15:2 Biking Safely ——————

When you ride a bike, follow all safety rules. Obey traffic signs. If you have to ride in the street, ride in the same direction as moving cars. Use hand signals when stopping or turning.

FIGURE 15–2. Follow traffic signs when you ride your bike.

FIGURE 15–3. Use hand signals when riding a bike.

Stop

Left turn

Right turn

You can make choices to help prevent bike accidents. Think about the following.

What if a friend asks you for a ride on your bike? Your parents do not want you to allow others to ride your bike. You know that it is not safe for anyone to ride on the handlebars, the crossbar, or on the back. What should you say to your friend? Would you make a safe choice?

Suppose a friend asks you to ride to the park. To get to the park, you and your friend will need to cross two busy streets. Why should you ask a parent before you ride to the park?

FIGURE 15–4. You can practice safety rules to help avoid bike accidents.

FIGURE 15—5. You can use a hand pump to inflate your bike tires.

15:3 Caring for Your Bike

You can prevent some accidents if your bike is in good condition. Make sure the brakes work well. All moving parts of your bike should be oiled every few months. Make sure there is a chain guard on your bike. Check the tires to see if they are filled with enough air. If you must add air, use a hand pump. Service stations have air pumps that are more powerful than a hand pump. Have a grown-up show you how to use this kind of pump. If you do not use it the correct way, the tire could explode and harm you.

Make sure the seat of your bike is adjusted for your height. Wear a helmet when you ride. Make sure your shoelaces are tied and your pant legs are not too loose. They can become caught in your bike's chain. Avoid biking after dark. If you must ride after dark, wear light-colored clothing, and have reflectors on your bike.

ACTIVITY

A Safe Bike

Look at the picture of this bike. Give a safety rule about each of these parts of the bike—chain guard, brakes, tires, reflectors, seat, and handlebars.

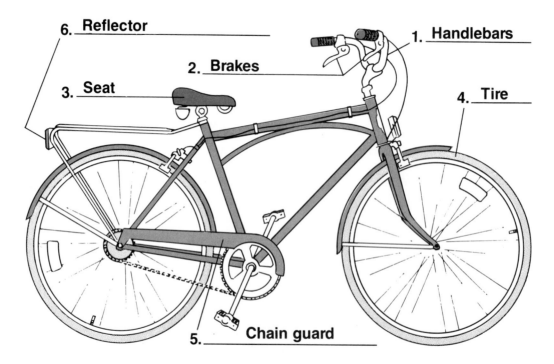

6. Reflector

1. Handlebars

2. Brakes

3. Seat

4. Tire

5. Chain guard

Think About It

1. What can you do to be safe when you ride on a bus?
2. In what direction should you ride when biking in the street?
3. How can keeping your bike in good condition help prevent an accident?

Safety in Your Community

People need to be aware of how to stay safe. Following safety rules is important for good health. You can learn rules that will help keep you and others safe in your community.

15:4 Poison and Safety

A **poison** is a substance that can harm you when it enters the body. Poisons cause many accidents in the home.

Some poisons might be swallowed. For example, a person may swallow a liquid from a container that has no label. The liquid may be a poison. Death or serious injury can result. Some poisons may be inhaled. Inhaling a poison may cause illness.

You can help prevent poisoning. Follow these safety rules.

- Do not remove labels from containers. Labels let you know what is inside each container.
- Carefully follow all directions on the labels.
- Keep all medicines and other substances that contain poison in safe places. Keep them away from young children.

FIGURE 15–6.

Poisons should be stored in safe places.

POISON: ☠
KEEP OUT OF REACH OF CHILDREN.
CAUSES SEVERE BURNS ON CONTAC
READ BACK LABEL CAREFULLY.
NET WT. 12 OZ.

FIGURE 15–7. If someone is poisoned, call the Poison Control Center.

Suppose someone has taken something that has made them ill. You think it may have been a poison. Tell your parent or another grown-up right away. They will call the doctor or the Poison Control Center for help. A person at this center will explain what to do to help.

15:5 Safety in the Water

Most accidents around water happen because someone is not careful. Sometimes people slip or fall into water and are not able to reach safety. Sometimes, a person may dive where the water is too shallow.

It is important to know how to be safe in water. To do this, you should learn how to swim. Even if you know how to swim, you need to follow water safety rules to avoid accidents. Practice safety when around any body of water. Follow rules around pools and other areas used for swimming.

Follow these rules whenever you swim.

- Swim only where it is safe. Be sure there is a lifeguard on duty or a grown-up nearby. Do not swim where a sign says *No Swimming*.
- Never go swimming alone. Always swim with another person.
- Do not swim if you hear thunder or see lightning. Lightning can strike the water and shock or kill you.
- Get out of the water if you feel tired or chilled. If you stay in water too long, you may not have energy to swim safely.
- Do not go in water over your head if you cannot swim well.
- Dive only in areas that are marked safe for diving. Diving in shallow water can cause injury to the head and neck.

FIGURE 15–8. Swim only when a lifeguard is on duty.

15:6 Safety from Strangers _____

Who is a stranger?

A **stranger** is someone you do not know well. Most strangers will not harm you or others. To be safe, you must follow safety rules around all strangers.

Suppose you are walking home from school. A stranger in a car drives up and offers you a ride. Do not go near the car. Walk or run in the opposite direction in which the car is headed.

What should you do if someone is following you?

Suppose you think someone is following you and you are not near your home. Look for a home with a special sign in the window. This sign will say Block Parent, Block Home, or some other safety title. The sign means that you can ask the person who lives there to let you inside if you think you are in danger. Know your neighborhood and where you can find a safe home.

FIGURE 15–9. A Block Parent home will have a sign in the window.

Suppose someone comes to your school. This person says your parent asked him to take you home. Should you believe him and go with him? You should always say NO.

Talk with your parents. Find out who has permission to take you home. Perhaps this person might give you a secret code word that only you and your parents know. Do not go anywhere with anyone if you are unsure about your parents' plans for you. It is always best to be safe.

Think About It

4. Why should labels be kept on containers?
5. Why should you get out of water if you are tired or chilled?
6. Why is it always best to follow safety rules around strangers?

Life Skills

▶ Always wear a safety belt when riding in a car.
▶ Use hand signals when turning or stopping on your bike.
▶ Make sure your bike has reflectors.
▶ Follow safety rules to prevent poisoning.
▶ Learn how to swim.
▶ Always swim where it is safe.
▶ Do not go with strangers.

Chapter 15 Review

Summary

1. You can help protect yourself from possible injury in a car by wearing a safety belt. *15:1*
2. Always follow safety rules when riding your bike. *15:2*
3. Keeping your bike in good condition can prevent some accidents. *15:3*
4. Poisons can harm a person if they are taken into the body. *15:4*
5. You can help keep safe if you swim only when a lifeguard is on duty or a grown-up is nearby. *15:5*
6. While most strangers will not harm you, it is important to follow safety rules around people you do not know. *15:6*

Words for Health

Complete each sentence with the correct word.
DO NOT WRITE IN THIS BOOK.

accident
poison
safety belt
stranger

1. A ____ can harm health if it enters the body.
2. Someone you do not know well is a ____.
3. A ____ protects you in a car.
4. An unexpected event that may cause injury for someone is an ____.

1. Why do most accidents happen?
2. What safety rules can you follow when riding your bike?
3. What should you check to keep your bike in good condition?
4. How can a poison get into a person's body?
5. How do you know when it is safe to swim?
6. What should you do if a stranger approaches you in a car?

Use the life skills from this chapter to respond to the following questions.

Situation: School is over for the day. As you leave school, someone you have seen around the neighborhood walks up to you. She says that she is to take you home.

1. What should you do?
2. Why should you avoid going with this person?

Find out what new safety features car makers are putting in cars. Find out how cars are tested for safety. Write about what you learn.

Caring for Injuries

Sometimes accidents happen even when you are careful. In case of injury, there are first aid steps you can learn to help yourself or others.

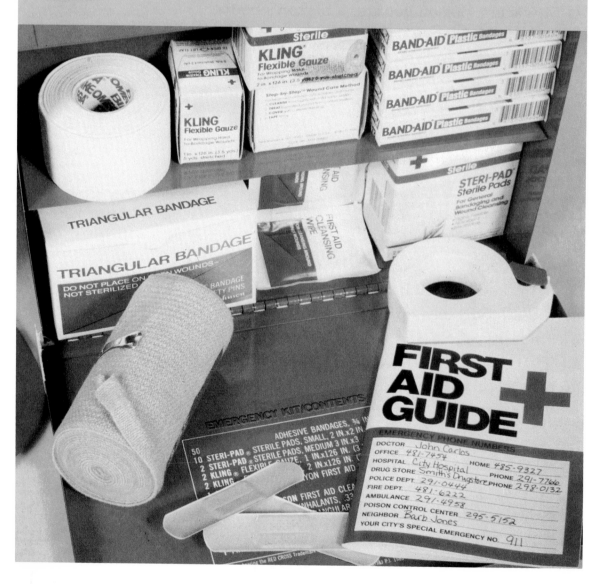

Chapter 16

STUDENT OBJECTIVES: You will be able to

- *discuss general rules for first aid.*
- *describe how to give first aid for common injuries.*

It is important for you to know what to do if someone becomes injured. Knowing facts about first aid may be important to you and others.

General First Aid Rules

Suppose you and a friend are riding bikes. Your friend falls and cannot move. He seems to be hurt badly. What could you do to help your friend?

16:1 Helping an Injured Person

A person who is injured may need your help. You should learn how to help an injured person. You can learn some rules to follow to help someone who is hurt.

Rules for helping an injured person

- Stay calm. You can think more clearly.
- Do not move a person who may be injured. Moving the person may make the injury worse.
- Comfort the injured person and say that you will get help.
- Get help quickly. Send a friend for help or yell for help. If you must leave, tell the injured person where you are going. Tell the person you will be back quickly.
- Cover the person. The person needs to stay warm.
- Remember the exact time of the injury.
- Try to remember everything that you saw.

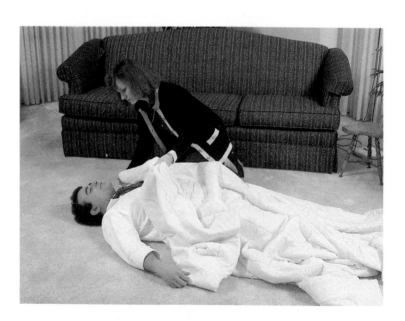

FIGURE 16–1. An injured person should be kept warm.

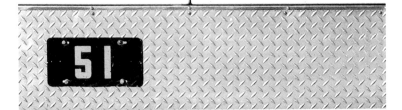

FIGURE 16–2. Dial 9-1-1 for help in an emergency.

16:2 Emergency Phone Calls ▬

What should you do in an emergency (ih MUR jun see)? An **emergency** is a situation in which help is needed right away. In an emergency, you may have to use the telephone.

What is an emergency?

Suppose your parent has an accident. No other grown-up is nearby. You must phone for help. What could you do?

- Some cities have an emergency phone number. It is 9-1-1. You can dial this number for police, fire, or medical help.
- You can also dial the number O. In this case, you will be talking to the phone operator. You can call the operator if you want police, fire, or medical help.
- Put other emergency numbers near each phone in your home.

When you call for help, tell the person who answers that there is an emergency. Speak clearly and calmly. Tell what has happened. Give the person your name and the place from where you are calling. Follow any directions the person gives you. Stay on the telephone until the person hangs up.

ACTIVITY

Making an Emergency Phone Call

Read the following situation. You and your mother are at home alone. Your mother falls down the stairs. She cannot move her leg. Working in pairs, practice what you would say to an operator when you dial for help.

Think About It

1. Why should you not move a person who has been injured?
2. Whom can you reach by dialing 9-1-1?

FIGURE 16–3. You should know how to make an emergency phone call.

214

Giving First Aid

At some time in your life, you may need first aid. You may need to give first aid to someone else. You can learn how to help yourself and others.

16:3 First Aid for Bleeding ___

First aid is the quick care given to a person who has been injured or suddenly becomes ill. You can learn to give first aid.

What is first aid?

One injury that may need first aid is a small cut. You should wash the cut with soap and water. Then, pat it dry. Cover the cut with a bandage. The bandage will help keep the cut clean. It will help keep germs from the injured area.

Suppose the cut is large and deep. Call for help from a grown-up right away. While you are waiting for help, you should start first aid treatment. Table 16−1 lists the steps for treating a cut.

Table 16−1

Treating a Cut
• Put a clean cloth over the cut.
• Press on the cut. Pressure on the cloth over the cut will help stop the bleeding.
• Do not remove the cloth.
• Get medical help.

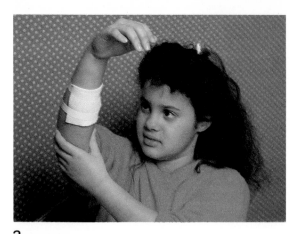

a

b

FIGURE 16–4. Raise a body part that is bleeding above the heart to help stop bleeding.

What is first aid for a nosebleed?

Look at Figures 16–4a and 16–4b. How is the person holding the hand that is bleeding? How is the person holding the foot that is bleeding? Any part of the body that is bleeding should be held higher than the level of the heart. When you raise the injured body part above the heart, you help stop the bleeding.

Nosebleeds can have many causes. An injury to your nose can cause a nosebleed. Blowing your nose often when you have a cold may cause a nosebleed. Cold weather dries out the inside of your nose. This may cause a nosebleed.

If you have a nosebleed, sit down and stay calm. Do not walk around, talk, or try to blow your nose. Doing any of this might cause the bleeding to increase. Pinch your nostrils shut for five to ten minutes. Breathe through your mouth. Cold cloths should be applied to your nose and face. Always tell your parent when you have had a nosebleed.

16:4 Broken Bones

Many injuries are caused by falls. Sometimes a person who falls may break a bone. A **fracture** is a break or crack in a bone. Sometimes a bone breaks and skin is not broken. This is called a closed fracture. An open fracture is a broken bone that sticks out of the skin.

Signs of a fracture include the following:

- The shape of the body part looks different than it did before the injury.
- There is swelling around the injury.
- There is pain when the body part is touched.

If you think someone has a broken bone, keep the person still. The injured body part should not be moved. More damage may occur. Call or go for help.

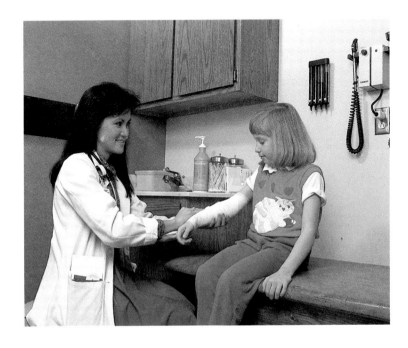

FIGURE 16–5. If you think someone has a broken bone, keep the person still.

FIGURE 16–6. Hot water can cause a burn.

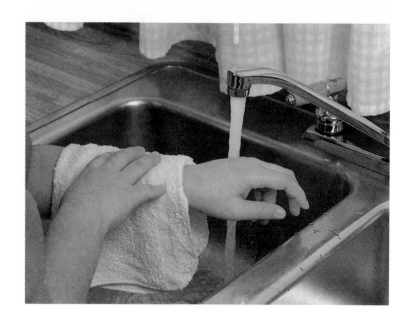

16:5   Treating Burns

Sometimes, people touch something hot and get a burn. Some burns are minor. A minor burn can be caused by contact with hot water, a hot pan, or steam. Follow these first aid steps for a minor burn.

- Place the burned area under cold water or run cold water over the burn. A cold, wet cloth can be loosely wrapped around the burn to help relieve pain.
- Pat the area dry.
- Place a dry, clean bandage over the burned area if needed.

Severe burns are more painful than minor ones. Severe burns can be caused by deep sunburns or by very hot liquid. Severe burns cause swelling and blisters. A doctor needs to treat any burn that is serious.

16:6 Stings, Bites, and Scratches

If a bee or wasp stings you, tell a grown-up right away. The bee's stinger may have to be removed from your skin. Run cold water over the area. The cold will help stop the pain.

Some people are allergic (uh LUR jihk) to certain kinds of insect stings or bites. To be **allergic** means to have a harmful reaction. A person who is allergic to insect stings or bites should have medical help right away if stung or bitten by an insect. This person should wear a necklace or bracelet that lets others know about his or her allergy.

Sometimes, pets and other animals may bite or scratch you. They may do this if they are playful or afraid. An animal's bite or scratch can cause an infection.

What does it mean to be allergic?

FIGURE 16–7. Be careful around all animals.

If bitten or scratched by an animal, follow these first aid steps.

- Wash the bite or scratch with soap and water.
- Apply a clean dressing.
- Get medical help.

Do not try to handle pets and animals that appear unfriendly or afraid. Handle all pets with care.

Think About It

3. Why should pressure be applied to a deep cut?
4. Why should a person who has a broken bone remain still?
5. What can cause a minor burn?
6. What can you do to help stop the pain of a bee sting?

Life Skills

▶ Help an injured person by staying calm, not moving the person, getting help quickly, and keeping the person warm.

▶ Know how to make an emergency phone call.

▶ Always wash a minor cut with soap and water.

▶ Keep a person still if you think a bone is broken.

▶ Learn first aid treatments for burns, insect stings and bites, and animal bites and scratches.

Health Highlights

Paramedic

There has been a bad accident. Two cars have come together on the road. People have been hurt. You can hear sirens and see flashing lights. An emergency medical vehicle is on the way. People are coming to help. Mike Smith is on the emergency vehicle.

Mike is a paramedic. He works for a hospital. He is trained to give emergency care to injured persons. Mike tries to help people at the scene of the accident. Injured people are then taken to a hospital to receive a doctor's care.

To become a paramedic, Mike took college classes for one year. He learned how to give first aid. He learned how to use equipment to help someone who is having a heart attack. He was trained to give drugs to help people who have been injured.

Mike enjoys his job as a paramedic. He likes using his first aid training to help other people.

Chapter 16 Review

Summary

1. There are rules to follow when helping an injured person. *16:1*
2. Making an emergency phone call correctly can help you give aid to a person who is injured. *16:2*
3. A cut should be washed with soap and water, patted dry, and covered with a bandage. *16:3*
4. A person with a broken bone should be kept still. *16:4*
5. A minor burn should be placed under cold water; a severe burn should be treated by a doctor. *16:5*
6. A person who is stung, bitten, or scratched may need medical help. *16:6*

Words for Health

Complete each sentence with the correct word.
DO NOT WRITE IN THIS BOOK.

allergic   first aid

emergency   fracture

1. The quick care of an injured or suddenly ill person is ___.
2. To be ___ means you have a harmful reaction to certain kinds of insect bites.
3. An ___ is a situation in which help is needed right away.
4. A ___ is a break in a bone.

1. Why is it important to stay calm in an emergency?
2. What are two emergency telephone numbers?
3. How should a nosebleed be treated?
4. What are signs of a fracture?
5. What is first aid for a minor burn?
6. What is first aid for an animal bite?

Use the life skills from this chapter to respond to the following questions.

Situation: You are playing basketball with your friend on the playground. The basketball hits your friend in the nose. Your friend's nose begins to bleed.

1. What is the first thing you would do for your friend?
2. What might you do to get help?

Make a first aid book. Include information about cuts, nosebleeds, broken bones, burns, stings, and dog bites. Describe what to do in each case. Include pictures in your book.

Community and Environmental Health

Did you know . . .

▶ your environment can affect your health?

▶ you can help protect your environment?

Health in Your Environment

Think about what you need to be healthy. You need clean air to breathe, food to eat, and water to drink. Sometimes air, food, and water are affected by pollution.

Chapter 17

STUDENT OBJECTIVES: *You will be able to*

- *identify ways your environment affects your health.*
- *describe how to protect the environment.*

Look around you. Think about what is around you. What do you see? What do you hear? What you see and hear can affect your health.

Pollution

When you walk or ride to school, what do you see? What kinds of buildings are along the way? What do you see in the streets and on the sidewalk?

17:1 The Environment and Your Health

Your **environment** (ihn VI run munt) is everything that is around you. It includes people, cars, buildings, lakes, and the air you breathe.

What is your environment?

Suppose the environment is dirty. There may be paper in the streets or smoke in the air. There may be trash in a lake. These problems can harm your health.

What is pollution?

Pollution (puh LEW shun) is products in the environment that can harm your health. Examples of pollution include trash, smoke, and loud noise. You increase your chances of getting sick when there is pollution where you live. A clean environment does not have pollution. A clean environment is healthful and safe.

FIGURE 17–1. Litter causes pollution on land and in water.

17:2 Litter

Litter is a kind of pollution. **Litter** is trash that is thrown away on land or in water. Litter can be paper, metal cans, plastic, glass, bottles, food, or worn-out clothing. It is against the law to throw litter in public areas.

Litter is not healthful. Litter can make people sick. There are more germs around dirty places with litter than around clean places. A person's chances of getting sick may increase.

Litter also can be a safety problem. Suppose you and your friends are playing in the park. A broken bottle is on the ground. What might happen if someone trips and falls on the bottle?

FIGURE 17-2. Waste products from factories can cause pollution.

17:3 Water and Air Pollution ⎯

Water pollution is products in the water that make it unclean and harmful. Water pollution can be caused in ways other than litter.

Sometimes, factories dump wastes into rivers, lakes, and streams. The wastes cause water pollution.

Sometimes, chemicals are put on fields where food is grown. Chemicals may be used to kill insects or to help the food grow. These chemicals leak into the ground. During a rain, the chemicals may wash into nearby rivers or lakes. The chemicals cause water pollution.

Pollution makes water unsafe to drink. Germs in the water can make people sick. Water pollution harms plants and animals that live in water. It would not be safe for people to eat animals from this water.

What is water pollution?

Air pollution is caused by harmful wastes in the air. This pollution may be caused by wastes from cars or smoke from buildings or factories.

Air pollution can harm parts of the body. It can get into a person's throat and cause a cough. It can harm lung tissue. It can increase heart rate. Air pollution also can make a person's eyes burn and water.

Laws have been passed to help stop pollution. Air and water must be checked to make sure they are clean. Factories are checked to make sure they do not cause water or air pollution.

How can air pollution harm the body?

 ## ACTIVITY

Your School Environment

Make a poster about keeping your school clean. List rules for doing this. Draw a picture of a clean environment for your school.

Think About It

1. Why should you try to keep your environment clean?
2. What can you do to help prevent litter?
3. How can water pollution affect your health?

Protecting Your Environment

People can find ways to avoid adding harmful products to land, water, and air. Think about what you can do to help make your environment clean.

17:4   Using Fuels Wisely

Everyone uses energy. You use energy when you turn on a light, ride in a car, or toast bread. Most energy comes from fuels. These fuels are found in the environment. Oil, coal, and natural gas are some fuels.

Fuels are burned to provide energy for heat. Fuels are burned to make electricity. Some waste products that are left over from burning fuels make pollution.

FIGURE 17–3. Some people use less fuel by using solar energy.

There are ways to burn fewer fuels. People try to use less coal, oil, and natural gas to heat their homes. They use less fuel to run their cars and factories. They turn off objects that use electricity when the objects are not being used. By burning less fuel, we protect our environment.

What are ways to burn less fuel?

17:5 Recycling

Besides making laws and using energy wisely, you can help protect your environment in another way. Some products can be recycled. To **recycle** is to use again. Products made from glass and aluminum do not have to be thrown away. They can be reused. Paper can also be reused. Recycling products made from paper, glass, and aluminum helps protect the environment. What can you do to help recycle these products?

Think About It

4. How can you use less fuel for energy?
5. How can you recycle products to protect the environment?

Life Skills

► Do not litter.
► Use less fuel to help protect the environment.
► Recycle products such as glass, paper, and aluminum.

Health Highlights

Noise Pollution

Noise is loud sounds. Noise can become a problem in the environment. Loud noise is a kind of pollution.

People need to be aware of harmful noise. People who live near airports often hear the noise a jet makes. People who are around loud noise may lose their hearing. Noise made by machines in some work places can be harmful to workers. People who work near very loud noises must wear ear protection.

Some people wear headphones. Sometimes, they turn the sound up very loud. People who listen to music in this way may lose some of their hearing.

People who wear headphones as they walk or jog outdoors can harm their health in another way. These people may not hear cars or trucks coming along the street. Sometimes, they cause accidents.

Be aware of loud noise. You need to protect your hearing.

Chapter 17 Review

Summary
1. Your environment affects your health. *17:1*
2. Litter is a kind of pollution. *17:2*
3. Water and air pollution are harmful to health. *17:3*
4. Fuels used for energy can be used more wisely. *17:4*
5. People can recycle certain products to help protect the environment. *17:5*

Words for Health

Complete each sentence using the correct word.
DO NOT WRITE IN THIS BOOK.

environment
litter
pollution
recycle

1. Trash that is thrown away on land or in water is ____.
2. ____ is products in the environment that can harm your health.
3. Everything that is around you is your ____.
4. To ____ is to use again.

Reviewing Health

1. How can your environment affect your health?
2. What are examples of litter?

3. What is one cause of air pollution?
4. What are three examples of fuels?
5. What products can you recycle?

Use the life skills from this chapter to respond to the following questions.

Situation: You and a friend are walking home from school. Your friend throws a piece of paper on the sidewalk.

1. What might you say to your friend?
2. Why is it important not to litter?

1. Do this experiment to show that there is dirt in the air. Place two jars outdoors. Place white cotton in each jar. Cover one. Keep the other one uncovered. Leave it outdoors for three days. After this time, observe the cotton. Write down the changes that you notice.
2. Make a list of ways your family can save fuels used for energy in your home. Discuss this list with other family members. Write down what changes your family agrees to make.

Glossary

A

accident: something unexpected that happens and may cause injury

agility (uh JIHL ut ee): the ability to change directions quickly

alcohol: a harmful drug found in some drinks

allergic (uh LURR jihk): having a harmful reaction

antibody (ANT ih bahd ee): a substance in your blood that kills germs

arteries: blood vessels that take blood away from your heart

B

bacteria: (bak TIHR ee uh): one-celled germs

balance: the ability to keep from falling

blood vessels: tubes that carry blood

C

caffeine (ka FEEN): a stimulant drug found in chocolate, coffee, and some tea and soft drinks

cancer: a disease in which harmful cells in the body grow in number and attack healthy cells

carbon dioxide: a gas that is a waste product of your cells

caring: showing love to others

cavity (KAV ut ee): a hole in a tooth caused by the germs in plaque

cell: the smallest part of a person's body

circulatory (SUR kyuh luh tor ee) **system:** the body system made up of organs that move blood throughout your body

cocaine (koh KAYN): a stimulant drug that comes from the coca plant

community (kuh MYEW nut ee): the place where you live

consumer: a person who buys and uses products and services

cooperate (koh AHP uh rayt): to be willing to work together with others

coordination (koh ord un AY shun): the ability to use more than one body part at a time

crack: a form of cocaine

crown: the part of a tooth you can see

cure: to make well

D

dental floss: a special thin thread used to clean between teeth

depressant (dih PRES unt): a drug that slows down the work of body organs

dermis (DUR mus): the inner layer of skin

diet goals: guidelines for eating to help you live longer and more healthfully

digestion (di JES chun): a process that changes the food you eat so it can be used by your body

digestive (di JES tihv) **system:** the body system made up of organs that help your body use food

disease: a condition of your body that keeps it from working as it should

drug: a chemical that changes how your body works

drug dependence: a need to continue to use a drug

E

emergency (ih MUR jun see): a situation in which help is needed right away

enamel (ihn AM ul): a hard, white covering that helps protect the crown of the tooth

energy: the power that helps your body work

environment (ihn VI run munt): everthing that is around you

epidermis (ep uh DUR mus): the outer layer of skin

F

family: the group of people to whom you are related

fiber: a material in food that helps wastes move through the body

filling: material that fills the hole in a tooth

first aid: the quick care given to a person who has been injured or suddenly becomes ill

fitness skills: actions that help you do physical activities

flexibility (flek suh BIHL ut ee): the ability to bend and move easily

fluoride (FLOOR ide): a substance that helps make teeth stronger and less likely to have cavities

food label: a listing of the ingredients found in a food

fracture: a break or crack in a bone

G

germs: very tiny living things

goal: something toward which you work

gum: the pink tissue around a tooth

H

harmful stress: stress that causes changes in the body that can harm health

health: the condition of your mind and body and how you get along with others

health behavior contract: a written plan that helps you practice a life skill

healthful behavior: an action that is healthful for you and others

healthful stress: stress that causes body changes that help you perform well

heart disease: an illness that affects the heart

heart fitness: the condition of your heart and blood vessels

J

joint: the place where bones meet

L

large intestine: the body organ through which solid waste passes

law: a rule that tells you and others in your community how to act

life skills: healthful behaviors to learn and to practice all your life

litter: trash that is thrown away on land or in water

M

marijuana (mer uh WAHN uh): a harmful drug made from parts of the cannabis (KAN uh bus) plant

medical checkup: an examination of your body in which the doctor gains information about your health

medicine: a drug used to treat an illness or injury

mouthguard: a device that covers the teeth to help protect them from injury

muscular endurance (MUS kyuh lur ihn DOOR unts): the ability to use your muscles for a long time

muscular strength: the ability of your muscles to lift, pull, and push

muscular (MUS kyuh lur) **system:** the body system made up of all the muscles in your body

N

nervous (NUR vus) **system:** the body system made of organs that control all your body actions

nicotine (NIHK uh teen): a stimulant drug found in tobacco

nutrient: a material in food that helps your body work as it should

O

oil gland: a gland that makes body oil

organ: a group of tissues that work together to do a certain job

over-the-counter (OTC) drugs: drugs that can be bought without an order from a medical doctor

oxygen: a gas needed for you to live

P

permanent teeth: your second set of teeth

perspiration (pur spuh RAY shun): the salty liquid waste that comes out of your skin

pharmacist (FAR muh sust): a person who prepares medicine for you

physical fitness: the condition of your body

plaque (PLAK): a sticky material that forms on teeth

poison: a substance that can harm you when it enters the body

pollution (puh LEW shun): products in the environment that can harm your health

posture: the way you sit, stand, and move

power: the ability to use strong muscles

prescription (prih SKRIHP shun): a written order for a medicine

primary teeth: your first set of teeth

pulp: the center of a tooth

R

reaction time: the amount of time it takes your muscles to respond to a message from your brain

recycle: to use again

refusal skills: ways you can say NO to behaviors or situations that are harmful for you and others

respectful: showing others you think what they say and do is important

respiratory (RES pruh tor ee) **system:** the body system made up of organs that help you use the air you breathe

responsible: acting in ways that show others they can depend on you

responsible decision: a choice that helps you have good health

responsible decision-making model: a list of steps you can use to make choices that lead to good health

root: the part of the tooth under the gum

rule: a guideline for you and others to follow

S

safety belt: a strap in a car that keeps you from being thrown from your seat

saliva (suh LI vuh): a liquid in your mouth that softens food

scalp: the skin that covers the top of your head

self-concept (KAHN sept): the way you feel about yourself

side effect: an unwanted body change caused by a medicine

skeletal (SKEL ut ul) **system:** the group of organs in your body that give your body support and shape

skin: the organ that covers your body

small intestine: an organ that breaks down most of the food you eat into substances your body cells can use

smokeless tobacco: tobacco that is placed in the mouth rather than smoked

speed: the ability to move fast

stimulant (STIHM yuh lunt): a drug that speeds up the action of body organs

stranger: someone you do not know well

stress: the response to any demand on your mind or body

symptom (SIHM tum): a signal that you may be sick

system: a group of organs that work together to do a certain job

T

tar: a brown, sticky substance in tobacco that is harmful

tissue (TISH ew): a group of cells that do the same kind of work

tobacco: a plant that contains the harmful drug nicotine

tooth X ray: a picture of the inside of a tooth

treatment: a plan to follow to improve your health

U

understanding: to care about how others feel

V

vaccine (vak SEEN): a substance made with dead or weak germs

veins: blood vessels that bring blood back to your heart

virus (VI rus): the smallest kind of germ

Index

medical checkup, **183,** 184
medical doctor, 120-121, 156
medicine, 116-117, **118,** 119-127
mental health, 2-25
milk, 75
mouthguard, 190
muscles, 50, 54-55, 93-95; illus., 54
muscular endurance, 92, **93**
muscular strength, 92, **93**
muscular system, 54, 55

N

nails, 177-178
nervous system, 59, 60-61, 85
nicotine, 144, 145
noise pollution, 233
nosebleed, 216
nutrients, 74
nutrition, 25, 70-85

O

oil gland, 176
organ, 51, 60
others food group, 77
over-the-counter (OTC) drugs, 119, 120
oxygen, 65

P

paramedic, 221
pediatrician, 191
permanent teeth, 185
perspiration, 175
pharmacist, 121, 127
Physical Best, 97-98
physical fitness, 90, **91,** 92-101, 105-110
physical health, 6
plaque, 187
poison, 203, 204
polio, 165

pollution, 227, **228,** 229-230
posture, 178, 179
power, 108
prescription, 120, 121
prescription drug, 121
President's Challenge, 97-98
primary teeth, 185
pulp, 186

R

reaction time, 107
recycle, 232
refusal skills, 12
respectful, 33, 42
respiratory system, 65, 66; illus., 65
responsible, 35, 42
responsible decision, 10, 11-12; 143, 149
responsible decision-making model, 11
rest, 179
root, 186
rule, 36, 40-41

S

safety, 110, 123-125, 197-207
safety belt, 198
saliva, 62
Salk, Dr. Jonas, 165
salt, 82
saying NO, 12, 135-137, 142-143, 147, 149
scalp, 177
school nurse, 43
self-concept, 8, 9-10, 12, 14
senses, 60
side effect, 125, 126
skeletal system, 52, 53; illus., 52
skills, 105-110
skin, 161, **174,** 175
sleep, 179

Photo Credits

Cover and frontispiece, George Anderson; **2, 3,** Dave Frazier/Photo Researchers; **4,** Doug Martin; **6,** Paul Brown; **7(l)** Doug Martin, **(r)** Aaron Haupt/Merrill; **8,** Doug Martin; **9, 11,** Ted Rice; **13,** Doug Martin; **18,** Bob Daemmrich/Austin, TX; **20,** Doug Martin; **21,** Hickson-Bender; **22-25,** Doug Martin; **28-30,** Bob Daemmrich/Austin, TX; **32,** Hickson-Bender; **33,** Alan Carey; **34,** Ted Rice; **35,** Mary Lou Uttermohlen; **37,** Doug Martin; **38,** Anne Schullstrom; **39,** Hickson-Bender; **40, 41,** Doug Martin; **43,** Elaine Comer-Shay courtesy Dr. Jo Ann Rohyens; **46-47,** Bob Daemmrich/Austin, TX; **48,** Hickson-Bender; **58,** Patrick Vielcanet/Photo Researchers; **61,** Doug Martin; **62,** Jack Sekowski; **67,** Doug Martin; **70-71,** Elaine Comer-Shay; **72,** Bob Daemmrich/Austin, TX; **74,** Alan Carey; **75, 76, 77, 80,** Elaine Comer-Shay; **81, 82, 83,** Doug Martin; **84,** Jack Sekowski; **85,** Ted Rice; **88-89,** Bob Daemmrich/Austin, TX; **90,** George Anderson; **92,** Doug Martin; **93(l)** Doug Martin, **(r)** Norma Morrison; **95,** Doug Martin; **96,** Lindsay Gerard/Merrill; **97,** Bob Daemmrich/Austin, TX; **101,** The President's Council on Physical Fitness and Sports; **104, 106,** Doug Martin; **107,** Norma Morrison; **109, 111** Doug Martin; **114-115,** Bob Daemmrich/Austin, TX; **116,** Doug Martin; **118,** Elaine Comer-Shay; **119,** Eric Hoffhines; **120,** Tim Courlas; **121, 122,** Mark Burnett/Merrill; **123,** Jack Sekowski; **124,** Mark Burnett/Merrill; **127,** Janet Adams; **130,** Doug Martin; **132,** Gerard Photography; **133,** File Photo; **134,** Traci Ostand/Merrill; **135,** Jeff Greenberg; **136,** Larry Day; **137,** Mark Burnett/Merrill; **140,** Larry LeFever/Grant Heilman; **142,** Image Workshop; **143,** Jeff Greenberg; **144,** Janet Adams; **145,** File Photo; **146,** Mark Burnett/Merrill; **147,** Image Workshop; **148,** Aaron Haupt/Merrill; **149,** File Photo; **152-153,** CNRI/Science Photo Library/Photo Researchers; **154,** Bob Daemmrich/Austin, TX; **156,** Doug Martin; **157,** Jack Sekowski; **158,** Syd Greenberg/Photo Researchers; **159,** Science Photo Library/Photo Researchers; **160,** Doug Martin; **161,** Eric Hoffhines; **162,** Doug Martin; **163,** Cecil H. Fox/Science Source/Photo Researchers; **164,** Pictures Unlimited; **165,** Historical Picture Service; **168-169,** Doug Martin; **170,** Bob Daemmrich/Austin, TX; **172,** Taylor/Light Images; **174,** Alan Carey; **175,** Studio Ten; **176,** Hickson-Bender; **177, 178,** Doug Martin; **182,** Bob Daemmrich/Austin, TX; **184,** Ted Rice; **185,** Doug Martin; **189,** Hickson-Bender; **191,** Ted Rice; **194-195,** Bob Daemmrich/Austin, TX; **196,** Aaron Haupt/Merrill; **198, 200,** Doug Martin; **201,** Ted Rice; **203,** Mark Burnett/Merrill; **204,** Doug Martin; **205,** Pictures Unlimited; **206,** Ed Zirkle/Image Broker; **210,** Mark Burnett/Merrill; **212,** Doug Martin; **213,** Ed Zirkle/Image Broker; **214, 216, 217, 218,** Doug Martin; **219,** Doug Martin; **221,** Alan Carey; **224-226,** Aaron Haupt/Merrill; **228,** Russ Lappa; **229,** File Photo; **231,** Frank Balthis; **233,** Brian Heston.

4 5 6 7 8 9 10 11 12 13 14 15—00 99 98 97 96 95 94 93 92 91 90